"In a world where so many peop and what their purpose is, author I subjects in a brilliant way to help u. _____ ___ ___ __ p___ __ __ ___ given identity. Through sharing the stories of Biblical characters who were plagued with moral failure, tainted reputations and sin, we see the importance of our identity being found in our Creator and not our past failures and sin. The material in this book can be used for small groups or personal reflection."

-James and Nancy Kilgore-Pastors,

Life Church Houston Texas

"As Women, we all struggle to find our identity, purpose and destiny. Are we called to be more? When everything goes wrong, where's God? These are just some of the questions that have been asked by women from the beginning of time.

This book is an invitation for self-discovery. Reflecting on your past mistakes and failures will help you peel back the layers of self-doubt and will give you the courage to move forward. You will see yourself though God's eyes by studying the lives of ordinary people, their struggles, and victories. You will see how they overcame, withstood many challenges during their lifetime, made a difference, and stepped out in faith to pursue their destiny and to find their purpose."

-Jeanne Hryhorchuk

Coordinator, Ima's Home for Children,

Life Church Houston Texas

"Working with women from hard places and seeing how heavily it weighs on them is very challenging. The Book of You guided these beautiful ladies through a self-discovery of who they are and were made to be. Her book illustrates God's true love for us as women and our purpose despite our pain. The book had a profound impact and helped transform the ladies' view of themselves. Ericka has a true heart for women and helping them see the beauty in each of them. This bible study is applicable for any woman who struggles to see their true worth and value."

-Dior Burns

Director, Family Hope Center,

Buckner Children & Family Services, Houston Texas

"I am honored that I had the opportunity to be a part of such a Dynamic Bible Study that took me on the journey of "THE BOOK OF YOU". I hope the power and the anointing from whence this book was written will inspire your faith walk. I saw a bit of me in all of these women of faith. The Protector, The Pleaser, The Instructor, The Mother and The Queen. Blessings to this great author for allowing God to use her in a way that will bring healing, empowerment and self-awareness. I think it will also serve as a great read for the man who is seeking to understand the creation and the design of God concerning His Daughters."

-Janet Booker

Overseer of Faith Deliverance Full Gospel Ministries,

Houston Texas

THE BOOK OF
YOU

THE BOOK OF
YOU
Discovering Your God Story

ERICKA P. GREENE

Trilogy Christian Publishers A Wholly Owned Subsidiary of Trinity Broadcasting Network 2442 Michelle Drive Tustin, CA 92780

Rights Department, 2442 Michelle Drive, Tustin, CA 92780.

Trilogy Christian Publishing/ TBN and colophon are trademarks of Trinity Broadcasting Network.

For information about special discounts for bulk purchases, please contact Trilogy Christian Publishing.

Trilogy Disclaimer: The views and content expressed in this book are those of the author and may not necessarily reflect the views and doctrine of Trilogy Christian Publishing or the Trinity Broadcasting Network.

Manufactured in the United States of America

10 9 8 7 6 5 4 3 2 1

Library of Congress Cataloging-in-Publication Data is available.

B-ISBN#: 978-1-64773-434-3

E-ISBN#: 978-1-64773-435-0

Dedication

This is dedicated to each person who encouraged and invited me to write what God placed in my heart – each serving as the paper and the ink for our shared stories.

Acknowledgments

To my husband, Rodney, who provided support, honesty, and strength throughout this process. To my mother, Brenda, and sister, Tameka, who always believed in me. Lastly, to our circle of seven – Melanie, Arielle, Jossalyn, Kaitlin, Danita, and Tarsha – I love you.

Introduction:
Our stories?

One day while listening to the Bible while driving to work, I decided to start with the first book of the New Testament, Matthew. As the voice began to read Chapter one, I must admit, I soon zoned out as the reader began to list all the generations of Jesus Christ –fathers to sons, beginning with Abraham. Yet this morning, something caught my attention. Typically, these "begets" seem endless, listing the fathers and sons of each generation, yet this one was different. Sprinkled throughout were the names of five women among all these men. This was not the norm in similar genealogies in the Bible and I figured God mentioned each one by name for a reason....

> *[1] The book of the generation of Jesus Christ, the son of David, the son of Abraham. [2] Abraham begat Isaac; and Isaac*

begat Jacob; and Jacob begat Judas and his brethren; ³And Judas begat Phares and Zara of **Tamar***; and Phares begat Esrom; and Esrom begat Aram; ⁴And Aram begat Aminadab; and Aminadab begat Naasson; and Naasson begat Salmon; ⁵And Salmon begat Booz of* **Rahab***; and Booz begat Obed of* **Ruth***; and Obed begat Jesse; ⁶And Jesse begat David the king; and David the king begat Solomon of her that had been the wife* **[Bathsheba]** *of Urias; ⁷And Solomon begat Roboam; and Roboam begat Abia; and Abia begat Asa; ⁸And Asa begat Josaphat; and Josaphat begat Joram; and Joram begat Ozias; ⁹And Ozias begat Joatham; and Joatham begat Achaz; and Achaz begat Ezekias; ¹⁰And Ezekias begat Manasses; and Manasses begat Amon; and Amon begat Josias; ¹¹And Josias begat Jechonias and his brethren, about the time they were carried away to Babylon: ¹²And after they were brought to Babylon, Jechonias begat Salathiel; and Salathiel begat Zorobabel; ¹³And Zorobabel begat Abiud; and Abiud begat Eliakim; and Eliakim begat Azor; ¹⁴And Azor begat Sadoc; and Sadoc begat Achim; and Achim begat Eliud; ¹⁵And Eliud begat Eleazar; and Eleazar begat Matthan; and Matthan begat Jacob; ¹⁶And Jacob begat Joseph the husband of* **Mary***, of whom was born Jesus, who is called Christ.*

Matthew 1:1-16 (KJV)

In a time where women were considered either property or second-class citizens, God chose to include the names of five women in the genealogy of Jesus Christ, our Savior. Why in a time when women had no voice, little to no property, limited political or legal rights, and left at the mercy of a male dominant society? Why, when one's genealogy was only considered credible if verified by the bloodline of the male ancestors? Even more curious, is that these conspicuous women have background stories of questionable reputation, shame, fear, and guilt.

The truth is God, Himself, chose a body (*Psalm 40:6; Hebrews 10:6*) with a bloodline that included two discarded and childless widows, a professional harlot and spy, an adulteress pregnant by her lover, and a young maiden engaged to be married but pregnant by another. God intentionally included the ancestral blood of these women in the body that would be sacrificed to save the sin of the whole world (*Hebrews 10:10*).

By mentioning these five women, God wants women and girls to understand and know that our value is not tied to the circumstances and events of our lives. Our value is fixed and permanent in the mind and heart of God. Our purpose was ordained in His mind before you or I ever came to be. His plan for us *is* good (*Jeremiah 29:11*) and He *is* for us (*Joshua 1:9*). Nothing is lost or wasted in Christ, not even the worse of you or your life, for all things work together for good to them that love God, and to them who are the called according to his purpose (*Romans 8:33*).

It is not a question of whether you are called by God (*Matthew 22:14*). The question is can you trust the story for which God created you and submit to what He has written and is writing on the pages of your life, for He is the author and finisher of your faith (*Hebrews 12:2*).

So, I invite you to take a journey in time with me; to go back in time and meet these five women so inseparable from our Lord God; to hear the beat of their hearts, the fear of their souls, and desperation of their circumstances. Along the journey, we will encounter others, great men and women, and witness their steps of faith in the perfect will and power of our God. We will see that their value in God was never lost or decreased but used for His perfect will to impact our world and each of us individually.

> *The question is can you trust the story for which God created you and submit to what He has written and is writing on the pages of your life, for He is the author and finisher of your faith. Hebrews 12:2*

Their stories are our stories and in meeting them and seeing them as God sees them, I pray you will meet the true and priceless woman inside of you who God created for his special purpose and plan.

Before we begin our journey, I want you to commit these truths to your heart, mind, and soul.

God is not a man that He should lie.

God never changes.

God will never leave you or forsake you.

His promises are **yes** and **amen** in Christ Jesus

God loves you – no matter the what's, when's, who's, or how's of your story.

And the last one...God sees YOU (*Genesis 16:13*).

Table of Contents

Section 1
What is Your Name?

You must be careful. Care about calling

people out of their names, using racial

pejoratives and sexual pejoratives and all that ignorance. Don't do that.

Words have the power to seep into everything around you. I think they get on the walls; they get in your wallpaper, they get in your rugs and your up-holstery and your clothes, and, finally, into you.

– Maya Angelou

I will give them—within the walls of my house—

a memorial and a name

far greater than sons and daughters could give.

For the name I give them is an everlasting one.

It will never disappear!

Isaiah 56:5

Chapter 1
More than just a name

"Names are not always what they seem."

— Mark Twain, Following the Equator: A Journey
Around the World

There is great importance in the naming of a child. It can reflect how that person is seen and also the expectations and potential of the person in the future. In fact, often a name seems to "fit" the person so much that when we meet others with that same name, we often look for similarities between the two as if the name is a character trait or personality.

Is your name associated with a person, event, or memory?

Does your name "match" with how you view yourself?

Have you ever changed or wanted to change your name? Why?

The 'Other' Names

Sometimes it is not the name on our birth certificate that we identify with, but other names given to us throughout life. It is the nickname by which we are known, the name we are called by those with whom we associate.

Yet, there are other names that we bear that are never placed on a birth certificate, a paycheck, or used in everyday life. These are the names we may have heard once in our lives or several times, but these names have a great impact on how we see ourselves. These names are often negative and associated with feelings of shame, guilt, or anger. Whether we choose to accept these names or not, these names can still cause pain and make us question who we are.

What other names or nicknames have you been given?

Did these names affect how you saw yourself or how others saw you?

Do you believe that a name 'makes' a person or does the person 'make' the name?

Jacob the "Cheater"

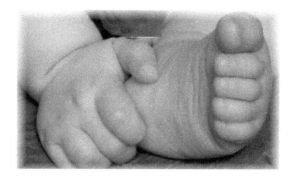

Jacob was the second born of a set of twins. Actually, he was the grandson of Abraham and the son of Isaac. Before the twins were even born, God told his mother, Rebekah, that the older would serve the younger and be a stronger nation of people (*Genesis 25:20-26, New Living Translation ("NLT")*).

Esau was born first and was described as a hairy, red baby, thus Esau in Hebrew means red and his descendent were Edomites ("edom" for "red"). Jacob, being the second born, was named for grabbing Esau's heel from the womb. Jacob in Hebrew means to "supplant" or "catch by the heel." Other translations describe a *supplanter* as one who moves in or replaces (Genesis 19:24).

The children were named according to how they were viewed at birth before they could walk or talk.

Read the description of Jacob and Esau in *Genesis 25:27-34.*

How would you describe Jacob and Esau's personalities or character traits?

It would seem that their names matched their personalities. Whether it was the effect of their names or not, Jacob became the "cheater" and Esau became the "red" hot head.

So, there is something in a name –whether it is a memorial, a prophecy, a blessing, or even a curse, no matter what your name is, it is more than just a name. It may affect or mark the nature and course of your life, the choices you make, and the choices made for you.

In fact, when we read further in Genesis 27, we find that not only does Jacob take Esau's birthright as the firstborn. He later deceives their father and obtains Esau's blessing. The twins' mother Rebekah actually tells Jacob how to deceive their blind father, Isaac, to get his elder brother's blessing.

Read *Genesis 27:1-10.*

The Blessing transcended the material wealth of one's inheritance. It declared and prophesied blessing over their abundance, their position, and their influence. So, Jacob took Esau's birthright (inheritance) and his blessing (his future)! Jacob truly took on the identity of his birth name.

Esau exclaimed, "No wonder his name is Jacob, for now he has cheated me twice. First he took my rights as the firstborn, and now he has stolen my blessing. Oh, haven't you saved even one blessing for me?" Genesis 27:36

Read *Genesis 27:28-29* and *Genesis 27:39-40.*

How did the blessing Isaac gave to Jacob compare to Esau's blessing?

Does Jacob deserve this blessing? Does Esau deserve his blessing?

Why would God allow Jacob to get the birthright and blessing? Why didn't He stop Jacob from successfully deceiving his brother?

Jacob's given birth name reflected how he was viewed and how he was treated. The course of his life followed the pattern of this identity.

Yet despite Jacob's deceptive ways, he was blessed. He became quite wealthy and influential. For although the way he obtained the birthright and blessing was not in God's will, the name and purpose given to Jacob by God were fixed.

No matter how you have been identified or named, God determines your name and future before you were born. Yet, we often have a name or have acquired an identity that is the opposite of who we really are in God. It is this name and identity that we accept as true and we live a life that seems to match it. Yet, like Jacob, your identity and purpose may look nothing like what God has declared, and what God declares is fixed.

A New Name

After Jacob's deception, he had to flee to avoid the deadly wrath of Esau. His mother sent him to stay with her brother, Laban, who was as deceitful as his sister and his nephew, Jacob. Laban deceived Jacob by tricking him to work double the time he intended and by marrying Laban's two daughters instead of the one he loved…yet Jacob prospered. His wives fought and brought strain to him…yet Jacob prospered. Laban became jealous and tried to deceive Jacob out of his wealth and family…yet Jacob prospered.

Nevertheless, Jacob was still the "cheater," a fugitive in another land, and separated from his family and his future. Yet God never forgot what he declared about Jacob to Rebekah when he was still in the womb. In order to claim his true identity and purpose, Jacob had to return and face who he was and what he did (*Genesis 31:3*).

On his way back to his land and family, he sends gifts to Esau in order to gain mercy as Esau is heading his way! For fear of Esau's wrath, Jacob sends his wives and children a different way to avoid their deaths, but before he faces Esau and his father, he must face his God.

Read *Genesis 32:24-28*.

Jacob had to struggle with who he was and who God created him to be.

Jacob was already blessed. He was blessed by his own doing and deceptive ways, yet at a point when all of his skills and wealth could not save him, he desperately wanted the blessing from God, a blessing that doesn't bring the pain of being a "Jacob."

Yet in order to obtain God's blessing and walk in his God-given destiny, he had to confess his birth name and all that this name represented. Only then, did God give him his true name, Israel. This name represented Jacob's true identity and the purpose and destiny which was tied to it…to birth the nation of Israel.

You have a name and purpose chosen by God before you were born. Life, people, events, our sins, can distort our identities and influence the direction of our lives. Yet what God has declared over you is fixed and does not change.

How do we find out who we really are and what our purpose is while struggling with our perceived identity and how others see us and treat us?

Like Jacob, we must relinquish our past and the identity that was never meant for us. This includes confession and repentance for the choices we have made, making amends to those we have mistreated, and forgiving those who have mistreated us.

We must reject the identity that is not of God. We must believe God's declaration of who we are in Him. We must believe God to such a degree that we relentlessly pursue God for the revelation of our God-given identity and the blessing that comes from it. We must hold on with a desperate faith and not let go until He breaks off the distorted identity from us and gives us our identity and purpose that are ordained before time.

Personal Application

Jabez

> *⁹Now Jabez was more honorable than his brothers, and his mother called his name Jabez, saying, "Because I bore him in pain."¹⁰ And Jabez called on the God of Israel saying, "Oh, that You would bless me indeed, and enlarge my territory, that Your hand would be with me, and that You would keep me from evil, that I may not cause pain!" So, God granted him what he requested.*
>
> *1 Chronicles 4:9-10*

Jabez was of the tribe of Judah and all we know is that his mother named him according to how his birth affected her. From his birth, he was known as the "one who causes pain." One can imagine how this impacted how he viewed himself, how he was viewed by others, and how this affected his future. For every time he heard his name, everywhere he went, he heard "you are a pain."

How many of us have felt that we were an inconvenience, irritation, or burden to someone in our lives? How many of us carry guilt and worthlessness for the pain we feel we have caused or represent to someone?

Yet Jabez did not accept his identity. He did not accept the small life that was forced upon him.

Unlike Jacob, Jabez did not change his name, his look, his clothes, his voice, or gain favor through deceit or self-sacrifice.

Jabez prayed to God. He prayed that God would grant him an identity and future, which were totally opposite to that of his name.

> His identity was a curse. He prayed for blessing.

> His identity limited his position and prosperity. He prayed for expanded influence and position.

> His identity left him isolated. He prayed for God's fellowship.

> His identity mandated that he continue to cause pain. He prayed for God to keep him from evil and pain, not only from others, but to keep him from causing pain in return.

Have the circumstances of your life caused great pain?

Have you caused great pain because of the pain you bear inside?

Give God your past, your name, your mistakes, your mistreatments, and don't believe a lie about who you are and what you are. Like Jacob, confess who you may have become and what you have done under that identity. Or like Jabez, reject that identity and claim your true identity and blessing from God who has been ready and willing "to grant your request."

The nations will see your righteousness, and all kings your glory; and you will be called by a new name, which the mouth of the LORD will designate. Isaiah 62:2

Chapter 2
Who are you and
why are you here?

From the story of Jacob and Esau, we know that the name or names we have been called often reflect how others view us in our lives. Whether our behavior or features choose our names, or our names influence our behaviors or features, there is an attachment to the name.

However, no matter what names you are called, there is still ***another name*** that speaks to who you are and who you are meant to be. It is your true name, the name that God calls you and the one given to you before you existed. It is this name that represents how God sees you, formed you, and for what purpose He created you. And this name and all it represents is fixed in the heart and mind of God. It is not altered by your circumstances, failures, accomplishments or success.

In fact, God offers a view as to how He sees you before you existed and before you had an identity or even a name.

> *26And God said, Let us make man in our image, after our likeness: and let them have dominion over the fish of the sea, and over the fowl of the air, and over the cattle, and over all the earth, and over every creeping thing that creepeth upon the earth. 27So God created man in his own image, in the image of God created he him; male and female created he them.*
>
> *Genesis 1:26–27*

Even before man existed, God declared man's identity and his purpose. God first revealed the essence of his creation. Essence is the intrinsic nature or character that cannot be changed. Most of us cannot distinguish an apple seed from other fruit seeds. No matter where or when you plant it, or even if you plant it, the essence will always be an apple seed, with an inherent ability to become an apple tree.

God declared the essence of man. Mankind is to be the very image of God, a reflection of who God is in intellect, creativity, person, and heart. Like an apple seed, the essence of who we are and for what we are made, is fixed whether it is realized or expressed. It is the "core" of who we are and what we are able to do. It existed before creation and cannot be changed.

God then declares mankind's purpose on Earth. Mankind was to have authority over creation, set it in order, and build upon it using his imagination and wisdom, based on the pattern and character of God. Like the apple seed, man's essence contained all that was necessary for him to perform this awesome purpose

Then, after God declared who man was (nature, character) and his purpose, did he create man and female (*Genesis 2:21-23*).

Before I formed thee in the belly I knew thee; and before thou comest forth out of the womb I sanctified thee, and I ordained thee a prophet unto the nations. Jeremiah 1:5

Even every one that is called by my name: for I have created him for my glory, I have formed him; yea, I have made him. Isaiah 43:7

Bookmark

The first mention of man's name, Adam, is when God has given him the task to start his purpose—naming the animals (*Genesis 1:19*). Adam in Hebrew means 'of the earth.' His name was tied to the object of his purpose and position, which was to have authority over the earth and all of its creatures.

So, the God who created the whole universe, knew you before you even existed. Moreover, He just didn't know you in a passive sort of "pass the next soul for the next baby in the assembly line" way. He declared your nature and purpose before you were conceived, already knowing all that your life would contain from beginning to end. He formed you on purpose for purpose, placing within you all that is needed to be the ordained person you were created to be.

What is your true name or what is your "essence"?

Why are you here or what is your purpose?

Understandably, these may seem like existential questions and hard to answer when we stop and think about them.

Some of us may answer quickly, not really giving it much thought.

"I am a child of God."

"I am a dedicated mother."

"I am blessed and highly favored."

"I am a _____." (*fill in the blank*)

Then there may be those who have their answer, those who know their identity and purpose from an early point in life or became aware of it after a life-altering event.

"I want to foster children."

"I want to become a lawyer and defend the abused."

"I want to share my story of struggle and triumph."

Some of us struggle with these questions, not really sure of our purpose, yet we are drawn to certain things or people.

"I think I'm meant to be a great mother."

"I feel I am called to encourage people."

Or

"I am meant to teach."

Does one of these descriptions apply to you?

Some of us have no answer. The responses listed above do not reflect who we really are, given all the layers that life has put on us and the many roles we play. Often our answers to these questions don't quite fit with all that we feel inside and with all the secret fears, dreams, and desires that reside within us.

For all of us, whether we have an answer or not, God has more to say to each of us. He has the answer.

For those who know their God-given identity and are walking in their calling, God still has more to reveal to you; to make sense of the things in your life that seem so opposite to your identity and calling; to enlarge your view of your destiny in spite of some of the things that possibly contradict your God written story.

For those who struggle with the answer of why they were born or have gone through what they have experienced, God has the answer for you, and it looks nothing like what you could ever imagine. Greater still, it is the truth.

For those who cannot allow themselves to believe that they are worthy of a God-given identity or purpose or who cannot trust God when their life has been anything but godly or blessed, God knows all and sees all, and His answer is the same.

God created you for a purpose and you are called to fulfill that purpose. So, whether you can believe it or see it, you are created with a God-ordained identity and purpose.

You and your life are not a mistake, mishap, or afterthought.

The psalmist declares that you are beautifully and wonderfully made, and no matter what has happened and where you may find yourself, He is there. His will for you is good. He has plans for you, plans to give you a future and a hope.

God is so committed to what he has ordained in you, He has already written a book of you and developed each chapter to document His presence in all the stages of your life and how His love and grace have sustained you for His purpose.

Like an open book, you watched me grow from conception to birth; all the stages of my life were spread out before you, [t]he days of my life all prepared before I'd even lived one day. Psalms 139:16 (The Message)

Are you ready to open up your book and discover your God story, the one He is writing for you, the one that rises above the pages of the story you have already accepted and believed about yourself?

Bookmark: Purposed for Expression. Silenced by Pain

Maya Angelou was born Marguerite Johnson on April 4, 1928. After her parents' marriage ended, she and her brother, Bailey (who gave her the name Maya) were sent to rural Stamps, Arkansas, to live with their grandmother. Although her grandmother helped her develop pride and self-confidence, Angelou was devastated when she was raped at the age of eight by her mother's boyfriend while on a visit to St. Louis. After she testified against the man, several of her uncles beat him to death. Believing that she had caused the man's death by revealing his identity, Angelou refused to speak for approximately five years.

In these five years, Maya read literature and poetry across genres, time periods, and cultures. When she finally spoke, she had a great capacity for poetic and provocative expression that provided her a platform to tell her story and that of so many others. From this platform she wrote the famous autobiographical work, "I Know Why the Caged Bird Sings" and numerous other famous works of poetic and prose expression. Today, she is heralded as one of the greatest American literary figures of our modern time.

The circumstances of her early life identified her as a mute and broken girl. Yet, this period of silence and pain was a time of preparation that transformed her to become the voice of a people – a voice of purpose.

https://www.notablebiographies.com/An-Ba/Angelou-Maya.html

Are you ready to accept His invitation to co-author your story by trusting Him and submitting all that you are, the good, bad, and ugly, to His plot? God is ready. He has been waiting for this moment to show you who you are.

"You may encounter many defeats, but you must not be defeated. Please remember that your difficulties do not define you. They simply strengthen your ability to overcome."

—**Maya Angelou**

author, poet, playwright, stage and screen performer, and director

Chapter 3
Identity and purpose

When life ends up totally different from what you imagined.

When dreams become nightmares from which you cannot wake up.

When you are betrayed, dismissed, abused, or left alone.

How do you define yourself? Who are you and why are you here?

Often, we see ourselves through the lens of what life has dealt us. We struggle with issues of self-worth and value when those expected to love us and care for us, do not. We battle with depression and anxiety, when life has thrown us curve balls that have pummeled us to the ground. We are left feeling useless and unimportant when it feels as if we are boxed in by a limited education, financial struggles, or chronic disease or disability.

Yet when we read God's word and what He says about who we are and what His plans are for us, we may secretly question the truth of that in our own lives given our circumstances.

I am fearfully and wonderfully made. Psalm 139:14

For I know the plans I have for you, plans to prosper you and give you a future and a hope. Jeremiah 29:11

When God tells us that He is right there with us in every circumstance no matter how dark and hellish, do you struggle with these verses in the midst of your pain and crisis?

No man shall be able to stand before you all the days of your life; as I was

with Moses, so I will be with you. I will not leave you nor forsake you.
Joshua 1:5

> *⁷I can never escape from your Spirit! I can never get away*
> *from your presence! ⁸If I go up to heaven, you are there; if I*
> *go down to the grave, you are there. ⁹If I ride the wings of the*
> *morning, if I dwell by the farthest oceans, ¹⁰even there your*
> *hand will guide me, and your strength will support me.*
>
> *Psalms 139:7-10*

Even if you do not doubt that God is there, have you struggled with the *why's* of your life?

"*Why* did he do that to me?"

"*Why* did they have to die?"

"*Why* am I still sick?"

"*Why* can I never get a break?"

"*Why* am I stuck in this situation?"

"*Why* is my ministry not growing?"

"*Why* am I alone?"

"*Why* did that happen to my family, my marriage, my child?"

In fact, our answer to those questions often reflects how we see ourselves and define our identity, and even how we believe others define us.

Tamar: "They Call Me Poison"

The story of Tamar is limited to one chapter in Genesis of the Bible. It is conspicuously placed right in the middle of the story of Joseph, one of the twelve sons of Jacob and father to one of the twelve tribes of Israel. Yet this woman's story is just as important as the men from whom a nation was born.

Tamar was married to the oldest son of Judah, the fourth oldest son of Jacob, the grandson of Isaac, and the great-grandson of Abraham. She was in the right family and married to the right son. She was set. Set by the right family, husband, and future. From all viewpoints, Tamar was where she was supposed to be in life, but life is variable, and things change. Tamar's life was changed drastically by the loss of her husband, broken promises, and desperate actions.

> *⁶In the course of time, Judah arranged for his firstborn son, Er, to marry a young woman named Tamar. ⁷But Er was a wicked man in the Lord's sight, so the Lord took his life. ⁸Then Judah said to Er's brother Onan, "Go and marry Tamar, as our law requires of the brother of a man who has died. You must produce an heir for your brother." ⁹But Onan was not willing to have a child who would not be his own heir. So whenever he had intercourse with his brother's wife, he spilled the semen on the ground. This prevented her from having a child who would belong to his brother. ¹⁰But the Lord considered it evil for Onan to deny a child to his dead brother. So the Lord took Onan's life, too.*
>
> *Genesis 38:6-10*

Tamar's life was falling apart with all of its promise disappearing before her eyes. Twice a widow, motherless, and left with few options, it is not hard to imagine how Tamar must have felt. Tamar would have to wait for Judah's youngest son to marry her and provide children. Until then, she remained a widow unable to proceed with her life.

> *Then Judah said to Tamar, his daughter-in-law, "Go back to your parents' home and remain a widow until my son Shelah is old enough to marry you." (But Judah didn't really intend to do this because he was afraid Shelah would also die, like his two brothers.) So Tamar went back to live in her father's home.*
>
> *Genesis 38:11*

Although the scripture does not speak to what Tamar thought about these events, one can only imagine that she was challenged with issues of self-worth, her identity and her place in the world. Through no fault of her own, she was downgraded from a chosen wife to a dishonored widow and was now someone considered "poison" or unworthy of the life she thought was to be hers.

What does one do when your life takes a turn and you are no longer who you thought you would be or could be? How do you reconcile God's word when it says that His thoughts and plans toward you are peaceful and not evil, to give you a future and hope, when what you have experienced is the opposite of that?

For many who struggle with what life has become and what we expected it to be, we submit to our state, push through our lives, and make the best of it. We are the ones who are seen as quiet and shy or the opposite, as strong and unbreakable. Yet on the inside, we are handicapped by afflictions of low self-esteem, depression, guilt, anger, or bitterness.

Others may have turned away from God to seek their own answers and find identity and purpose in other things for which they feel they have control. Often this leaves them with more shame, emptiness, and disconnection

It is in this latter group that we find Tamar.

> *¹²Some years later Judah's wife died. After the time of mourning was over, Judah and his friend Hirah the Adullamite went up to Timnah to supervise the shearing of his sheep. ¹³Someone told Tamar, "Look, your father-in-law is going up to Timnah to shear his sheep."*
>
> *Tamar was aware that Shelah had grown up, but no arrangements had been made for her to come and marry him. ¹⁴So she changed out of her widow's clothing and covered herself with a veil to disguise herself. Then she sat beside the road at the entrance to the village of Enaim, which is on the road to Timnah. ¹⁵Judah noticed her and thought she*

was a prostitute, since she had covered her face.

¹⁶So he stopped and propositioned her. "Let me have sex with you," he said, not realizing that she was his own daughter-in-law.

"How much will you pay to have sex with me?" Tamar asked. ¹⁷"I'll send you a young goat from my flock," Judah promised.

"But what will you give me to guarantee that you will send the goat?" she asked. ¹⁸"What kind of guarantee do you want?" he replied.

She answered, "Leave me your identification seal and its cord and the walking stick you are carrying." So Judah gave them to her. Then he had intercourse with her, and she became pregnant. Afterward she went back home, took off her veil, and put on her widow's clothing as usual.

Genesis 38:12-18.

Out of desperation, despair, anger, or all three, Tamar took drastic action. She found her own solution to her problem. Through deceit and sin, she decided to no longer wait for others or even for God to provide.

It may be easy to judge or criticize Tamar for deceiving her father-in-law to engage in what is considered taboo and abominable. Yet how many of us have sought our own vindication for what we believed was taken away unfairly – whether a relationship, a reputation, health, or financial standing? If we are honest and take inventory of our lives, our answer to this question would be "yes." If we allow ourselves to take a deeper look, many will have to admit that we put ourselves at risk for tragic circumstances and greater loss by those actions.

Even if you have not sought self-vindication for a perceived wrong done to you, one can understand the betrayal and sense of rejection that Tamar must have experienced for no other reason than she married wrong, when she thought she married right.

In the time of Tamar, marriage was a legal, binding union to ensure the growth of a nation. In this culture, the first-born son inherited the most from the father, to ensure that the name of the family and their assets were preserved in right order within the family. However, if the firstborn died before conceiving children, then the next son in line was required to marry the widow and father a son that would be named after the deceased eldest brother. Further, that son would receive the greater inheritance even above that of his biologic father and brothers (*Deuteronomy 25:5-6*).

For women of that time, there were not many choices. A woman first lived under the protection and authority of her father and/or brothers and then by marriage, lived under that of her husband. Furthermore, a woman's value was tied to her ability to birth children, specifically sons, for her husband's legacy. Being unmarried and barren, was considered a great shame for a woman who was often left without alternatives from her limited life (divorce or grouped with other wives or concubines, poverty, or harlotry).

TAMAR: "Drinking the Poison"

Tamar was likely a young girl, under the age of 20. She was appropriate for marriage and obviously considered worthy to marry the firstborn son of a large, and by all measures of that day, a wealthy family.

Yet, the word of God provides a glimpse into how Tamar's identity was changed by circumstances out of her control.

> *Then Judah said to Tamar, his daughter-in-law, "Go back to your parents' home and remain a widow until my son Shelah is old enough to marry you."* (But Judah didn't really intend to do this because he was afraid Shelah would also die, like his two brothers.) *So Tamar went back to live in her father's home.*
>
> *Genesis 38:11*

She married a son who was evil before God and God removed him. She married his brother as custom required and he died also for selfish, and evil actions. Now, she was left to wait for a third husband, not yet a man.

Tamar, who was deemed worthy to birth the children for a respected family, was now considered as poisonous as a black widow spider. She was to be avoided, put aside and forgotten.

Forgotten. Put aside. Downgraded. Unworthy. Poison.

These labels or descriptions may not be printed on the shirts we wear or tattooed on our arms for display, but we may bear the scars of these and other labels 'tattooed' upon us by our experiences or by others who were close enough to make the first cut.

These hidden names and identities that we carry may not be evident to those around us but are expressed in how we view others, how we forgive, how we trust, where and to whom we seek refuge, and ultimately how we view ourselves and even our God.

Yet, God says you are fearfully and wonderfully made, and valued above creation (*Psalms 139:14; Matthew 10:39-41*).

[Yet we may struggle to see the value in others because we still struggle to see the value in ourselves. We cannot move forward in life for fear of failure. We fear we are inadequate, unequipped, unworthy to be more or do more.]

You are chosen as a royal daughter of great value with an ordained purpose (*1 Peter 2:9*).

[Yet we may struggle with stressors and challenges of everyday life, left without passion or an identified purpose to pursue.]

Yet, God says that He loves you with an everlasting love and remains faithful to you.

[Yet, we may struggle with loving others or trusting other's love, finding ourselves in and out of uncommitted and unfaithful relationships. Or we keep superficial connections, choosing the safety of "me, myself, and I," yet struggling with loneliness, isolation, and depression.]

Yet God says when others forsake you, He will never leave you (*Psalms 27:10*).

[Yet, we may forsake others for fear of being forsaken first. We avoid closeness and emotional intimacy for fear of rejection and abandonment. We expect disappointment and let down. We believe in God but not convinced He believes in us.]

Yet God says he will strengthen you and support you with his righteous hand (*Isaiah 41:10*).

[Yet, after we give it to God, we immediately take pick it back, to manage and fix in our own strength.]

Yet God says that He has begun a good work in you, and He will complete it in Jesus Christ (*Philippians 1:6*).

[Yet, we are content to remain at our level of faith-believing in God, trying our best, but not really experiencing the deliverance and victory over the issues of life.]

Do you struggle at times with the seeming contradiction of who you are suppose or desire to be and who you see in the mirror? Whether by your own choices or the consequences you have suffered from other's choices, you can find it difficult to see yourself as God declares when you look over your life or just look into a mirror.

Yet God does declare another identity: The identity He declared before we even existed. The Bible says that He saw your substance and fashioned your days in accordance with that substance.

Your eyes saw my substance, being yet unformed. And in Your book they all were written, the days fashioned for me, When as yet there were none of them. Psalms 139:16

Substance is defined as "the real physical matter of which a person or thing consist and which has a tangible, solid presence."

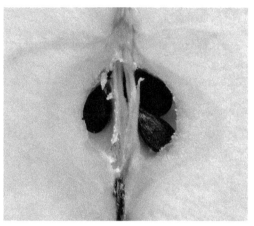

Under the layers of life's experiences that have defined you, is the substance that God, Himself, declared before time. It is this substance that carries the elements of your true identity in God and ultimately the seeds of your God-given purpose on Earth.

God says our days are already written in His book and He has fashioned each of those days in accordance with our identity and purpose.

In other words, God created a story about you that is unique to only you. Your story has a beginning and an ending and although the plot of your life may have unexpected twists and turns, He is not surprised. He knew, He prepared, and He is and has been there, eternally committed to the plans He has for you.

"For I know the plans I have for you," says the Lord. "They are plans for good and not for disaster, to give you a future and a hope." Jeremiah 29:11

Furthermore, He does not take it all back.

"For God's gifts and his call can never be withdrawn." Romans 11:29

So, whether we obey or disobey, live according to God's will or not, or even know God as Lord, our substance is fixed and is critical for the purpose for which you were made.

Tamar: The Purpose in the Name

Tamar made a choice. She would not be left undone. She was going to redeem the promise made to her no matter the risk or outcome.

> *²⁴About three months later, Judah was told, "Tamar, your daughter-in-law, has acted like a prostitute. And now, because of this, she's pregnant."*
>
> *²⁵"Bring her out and let her be burned!" Judah demanded.*
>
> *But as they were taking her out to kill her, she sent this message to her father-in-law: "The man who owns these things made me pregnant. Look closely. Whose seal and cord and walking stick are these?"*
>
> *²⁶Judah recognized them immediately and said, "She is more righteous than I am, because I didn't arrange for her to marry my son Shelah." And Judah never slept with Tamar again.*
>
> *²⁷When the time came for Tamar to give birth, it was discovered that she was carrying twins. ²⁸While she was in labor, one of the babies reached out his hand. The midwife grabbed it and tied a scarlet string around the child's wrist, announcing, "This one came out first." ²⁹But then he pulled back his hand, and out came his brother! "What!" the midwife exclaimed. "How did you break out first?" So he was named Perez. ³⁰Then the baby with the scarlet string on his wrist was born, and he was named Zerah.*
>
> *Genesis 38:24-30*

Despite her actions and sin, Tamar had no idea that she was created for a purpose. She was ordained before time to be the mother of Judah's children. It was not that God wanted her to be widowed, rejected, or betrayed. Nor is it that God justifies and allowed Tamar to sin to bring about His will. For God's will supersedes all other wills even in the face of sin and unrighteousness. Yet God remains righteous while judging what is right and what is not.

> *10"Therefore listen to me, you men of understanding:*
>
> *Far be it from God to do wickedness, and from the Almighty to commit iniquity.*
>
> *11For He repays man according to his work,*
>
> *And makes man to find a reward according to his way.*
>
> *12Surely God will never do wickedly,*
>
> *Nor will the Almighty pervert justice."*
>
> *Job 34:10–12*
>
> *For has anyone said to God, "I have borne chastening;*
>
> *I will offend no more; Teach me what I do not see;*
>
> *If I have done iniquity, I will do no more"?*
>
> *Should He repay it according to your terms, Just because you disavow it? You must choose, and not I;*
>
> *Therefore speak what you know.*
>
> *Job 34:33*

Tamar was made to survive and bring forth life in the form of two sons. She had no idea that all she endured was not because she was less than, unworthy, or even poison but because she was the opposite.

The name Tamar means "date palm tree," and like the palm tree, Tamar withstood and survived beyond the circumstances of her life. In the face of neglect, abuse, and death, she lived. She was bruised but was not broken and was strong enough to support and deliver life, in the form of her twin sons, Perez and Zerah.

Although, the Bible does not provide much of a follow up to her life and how she lived, based on the culture of that time and the word of God, Tamar would never be destitute or ashamed again. She would forever be cared for and protected by Judah as the mother of his children without the obligations of a wife (*Genesis 38:14-27*).

In fact, the same woman who was considered worthless and disposable, judged a harlot deserving of death, was proclaimed more righteous than them all.

"She is more righteous than I am, because I didn't arrange for her to marry my son Shelah." And Judah never slept with Tamar again. Genesis 38:26b

Yet her story does not end there.

Tamar never knew that her name, a name tied to great hurt and shame, would one day be listed among the great names of the Bible.

She never knew she was chosen to be in the bloodline of the Savior of the world as a genealogical "mother" to Jesus Christ.

She never knew that her story would be told as a testament to God's faithful purpose and plan.

What is your name? What is your substance?

But now thus saith the Lord that created thee, O Jacob and he that formed thee, O Israel, Fear not: for I have redeemed thee, I have called thee by thy name; thou are mine. Isaiah 43:1

Tamar's story in many ways is our story and God has blessed us with the ability to see His hand in her life. Her story is a witness to us that what God says and what God promises is true. It is true then; it is true now. It is true for me and it is true for you. It is true whether we submit to God in faith and obedience or turn away and trust ourselves.

Tamar and Jacob chose their own ways to obtain their promise. Jacob lived with the shame and consequence of his betrayal and wanton lust, placing his inheritance at great risk. Tamar submitted to her false identity by becoming "downgraded," "unworthy," and "poison" wrapped in the veil of a harlot and a deceiver. This resulted in more betrayal, shame, and scandal. It almost resulted in Tamar's death and the death of her unborn children.

Although the Bible does not provide further details, their choices may have limited their ability to fully experience the revelation of God's hand upon their lives.

Tamar did not understand that God was faithful to her purpose regardless of what was lost or broken.

Can you trust and believe that God has given you an identity and purpose despite how life has labeled you?

Tamar submitted to the false identity. She became deadly, downgraded, and dismissed. She believed the lie of this identity and acted under that identity.

Can you consider that the picture taken of you by life or choices is not the actual photo of who you think you are but the "negative image," the opposite image, of who you are ordained to become?

God wants to peel away that negative image and reveal to you who He sees when he looks at you, a wondrous and beautiful masterpiece created for good works and for His glory.

In order to do that, we must first allow God to remove the labels we have dutifully worn. We must reject the identity put upon us and take on Christ's identity, for we are made in His image and we belong to Him (*1 Corinthians 6:19*).

Even if you do not feel it, say it.

Even you cannot trust it, walk in it and "act out" from your

God-given identity.

Even if you fear it, ask Jesus to walk with you and show you and then let Him tell you who you are.

Pray that the Lord open your eyes to see past the false identity and discover who you really are and for what valuable purpose you were created. If for nothing else than to show God's faithfulness to your story on this earth.

"Everybody is trying to figure out who they are. The problem is most of us are expecting creation to tell us. We walk into the day with the expectation that a created thing (people, money, intellect, jobs, followers, etc.) can give us our names. But we all know that these things are fickle and susceptible to change therefore whatever identity they give us one day won't be the identity we're handed the next. Perhaps that's why we're all over the place, confused, and insatiably dissatisfied with what the mirror shows us. God is unchanging though, and His thoughts of us are consistent, thorough, true, and authoritative. Let Him tell you who you are, He's the only One who has the right to anyway." – Jackie Hill Perry

Chapter 4
A will within a will

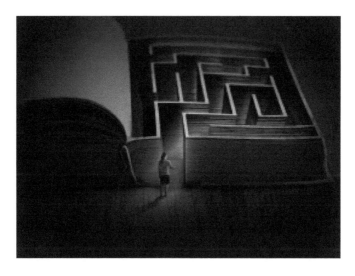

⁸My thoughts are nothing like your thoughts. And my ways are far beyond anything you could imagine. ⁹For just as the heavens are higher than the earth, so my ways are higher than your ways and my thoughts higher than your thoughts.

¹⁰The rain and snow come down from the heavens and stay on the ground to water the earth. They cause the grain to grow, producing seed for the farmer and bread for the hungry.

¹¹It is the same with my word. I send it out, and it always produces fruit. It will accomplish all I want it to, and it will prosper everywhere I send it. Isaiah 55:8-11

Indeed, before the day was, I am He;

And there is no one who can deliver out of My hand;

I work, and who will reverse it?

Isaiah 43:13

God's will and purpose is beyond our will and individual choices. His will is beyond our understanding. Our perspectives are so limited in comparison to the immeasurable, limitless, and perfect will of God Almighty.

We live in time, stages, and in sequence – one day after another; one event followed by a series of events. God is independent of time. He made time and knows the end from the beginning. As God, He sees all things "at the same time" whether it is the past, present, or future.

[10]I have seen the God-given task with which the sons of men are to be occupied. [11]He has made everything beautiful in its time. Also He has put eternity in their hearts, except that no one can find out the work that God does from beginning to end. Ecclesiastes 3:10-11

> *[9b]I am God, and there is none like me.*
>
> *[10]Only I can tell you the future before it even happens.*
>
> *Everything I plan will come to pass, for I do whatever I wish.*
>
> *[11]I will call a swift bird of prey from the east—*
>
> *a leader from a distant land to come and do my bidding.*
>
> *I have said what I would do, and I will do it.*
>
> *Isaiah 46:9b-11*

So how do we fit in God's will?

God created you with an identity and a purpose. The "substance" of you was made to serve God and His purpose. His will is to work His purpose through us and with us, as His children, made in His image and likeness.

For we are His workmanship, created in Christ Jesus for good works, which God prepared beforehand that we should walk in them. Ephesians 2:10

As discussed in Section 3, although Tamar was purposed to be in the lineage of our Lord and Savior, she chose to take matters into her own hands. She acted from a place of betrayal, low self-worth, and bitterness. She felt justified in her deception and sin, putting her life and the lives of her unborn sons at risk.

Tamar did become a mother and despite her tainted story, she was worthy to be named in the genealogy of Jesus Christ (*Matthew 1:1*). Yet was Tamar justified in her actions to obtain the promise or purpose of her life? Are we justified to seek what is "due to us" or resort to our own solutions, when life has treated us unfairly?

> *31 "For has anyone said to God, 'I have borne chastening;*
>
> *I will offend no more; 32 Teach me what I do not see;*
>
> *If I have done iniquity, I will do no more'?*
>
> *33 Should He repay it according to your terms, just because you disavow it? You must choose, and not I; Therefore speak what you know."*
>
> *Job 34:31-33*

Should God vindicate according to what we consider justice or what we believe to be right or do we submit to God's plans and purpose for us? Just as Tamar had a choice, we have a choice. We must choose between what we think about our life and what God thinks.

The answer is we should choose to trust God even when we cannot understand who we are and do not know our purpose. We must seek God for direction even as we face struggles that block our ability to see our worth or our God-given identity.

5 Trust in the Lord with all your heart, and lean not on your own understanding; 6 In all your ways acknowledge Him, and He shall direct your paths. Proverbs 3:5-6

What happens to our purpose when we serve everything else, including ourselves?

Although God's will always be accomplished, how we are used in His greater purpose is often dependent upon the choices we make. Yes, His plans for us are "good" and "not evil," but He has chosen to give us free will, with the ability to co-author our stories.

Whether we align with God or not, His greater purpose is fulfilled. The role we play in God's purpose will always be tied to our purpose. How we play that role will impact our personal lives and those close to us, yet we are still used of God to accomplish His will – either ending with great cost to us or a great crown for us!

The Nazarite Vow

A Nazarite was someone consecrated as Holy unto the Lord with specific vows to keep for a season or permanently.

The vows were to:

* never drink wine or strong drink;

* never cut one's hair; and

* never be near or touch a corpse even if it was family.

The Bible tells us of two such Nazarites whose beginnings were similar but whose endings were very different – Samson and Samuel.

Samson lived during the time when the nation of Israel had finally settled in the Promised Land. Before there were kings such as David or Solomon, there were judges who provided oversight and enforced the laws of God.

Samson parents were unable to have children. The angel of Lord declared that his mother would bear a son and he would be dedicated to God as a Nazarite (identity). She was told that her son would save Israel from the Philistines, an idol worshiping and violent nation, which oppressed Israel (purpose).

³The angel of the Lord appeared to Manoah's wife and said, "Even though you have been unable to have children, you will soon become pregnant and give birth to a son. ⁴So be careful; you must not drink wine or any other alcoholic drink nor eat any forbidden food. ⁵You will become pregnant and give birth to a son, and his hair must never be cut. For he will be dedicated to God as a Nazarite from birth. He will begin to rescue Israel from the Philistines."

Judges 13:3-5

Samson grew to be a mighty man with great strength and power. However, despite his natural gifts and God endowed power, he was immature, bad-tempered, and had a lust for women.

He killed a lion with his bare hands and later ate the honey from a nest of bees that settled in the corpse. He even fed his parents the honey and did not tell them from whence he got it.

He chose to marry a Philistine woman despite his parents' objection, demanding their consent and throwing himself a party (with strong drink) with 30 men of the Philistine nation.

Despite this, God used his strength and even those other less ideal qualities to overpower the Philistines on many occasions for the next 20 years.

His downfall was a woman named Delilah.

The Philistines bribed her with money to find out the source of his strength. After several attempts, Samson finally relented and told her it was his hair. While asleep, she cut his hair, and Samson was taken into captivity with his eyes gouged out. He remained a tortured slave for ten years, as God had removed His power from Samson.

Over time his hair grew back…

At the end of his life, while the Philistines were celebrating his down-fall and blaspheming the God of Israel, Samson prayed to the Lord one last time to restore his strength so that he could vindicate him-self and the Lord. God heard his prayer and gave him his powerful strength back. While propped between two large pillars that support-ed the temple where the Philistines were celebrating, Samson pushed down the pillars and the whole structure crushed and killed more Phi-listines at one time than all that Samson had killed before.

Samson's story ended with the defeat of the Philistines, as God in-tended. He was ordained before birth and created by God for this purpose, yet because of his choices, it was at great cost.

"Whatever you do, He will make good of it. But not the good he had prepared for you if you had obeyed him."

The Other Nazarite

Samuel was also the child of a barren woman, Hannah. Her husband loved Hannah, but his other wife taunted her for being barren. She pleaded with the Lord with much anguish and tears and vowed that if He granted her a child, she would consecrate Him unto the Lord to serve Him in His temple. In other words, she would give the child to the temple priest to be raised in service to the Lord for his whole life. God granted Hannah her request, and Samuel was born and consecrated as a Nazarite.

> *[10]Hannah was in deep anguish, crying bitterly as she prayed to the Lord. [11]And she made this vow: "O Lord of Heaven's Armies, if you will look upon my sorrow and answer my prayer and give me a son, then I will give him back to you. He will be yours for his entire lifetime, and as a sign that he has been dedicated to the Lord, his hair will never be cut."*

> *1 Samuel 1:10-11*

Unlike Samson, Samuel's life took a different path. He honored God by keeping his vow and served the Lord in righteousness.

[19]So Samuel grew, and the Lord was with him and let none of his words fall to the ground. [20]And all Israel from Dan to Beersheba knew that Samuel had been established as a prophet of the Lord. 1 Samuel 3:19-20

He obeyed God even when he initially did not understand and questioned God's command to reject King Saul, a disobedient self-centered man, and anoint David as the King of Israel, a man described as being "after God's own heart."

Now the Lord said to Samuel, "How long will you mourn for Saul, seeing I have rejected him from reigning over Israel? Fill your horn with oil, and go; I am sending you to Jesse the Bethlehemite. For I have provided Myself

Ericka P. Greene   57

a king among his sons." 1 Samuel 16:1

One story with great costs and another story with great gains, but in the end, both are heralded as great men of faith in the great chapter of faith in the book of Hebrews.

"How much more do I need to say? It would take too long to recount the stories of the faith of Gideon, Barak, Samson, Jephthah, David, Samuel, and all the prophets. " Hebrews 11:32

Your identity and purpose are ordained and declared by God before you existed. You are created uniquely for this purpose and it is God's will to accomplish it through you. However, how you respond to God's direction on your life can impact the role you play in God's grand design.

Your story is written in God's book and He wants you to co-author it with Him. In the end, the outcome He has chosen will prevail. Yet, you have the choice as to whether your character in the story loses or gains all that God has for you, for those connected to your life, and the generations yet to be born.

Personal Reflection

What role have you played in the story of your life?

Even if you have already given your life to Christ (*John 3:3-5*), have your choices or reactions reflected your trust and faith in God? Have your actions contributed to losses or missed blessings in your life?

If you have never really given your heart to Jesus, either believing He is the Son of God, and/or trusting Him as your Lord and Savior, have you ever wondered why you exist and the point of it all?

The fact that you are reading this suggests that you are looking for an answer or direction for your life. You may not have asked yourself these exact questions, but you sense a void and hunger inside that is desperate to be satisfied.

The God of your soul has ordained this time and season to meet you where you are and provide life for your soul (*John 6:35*).

First, He wants to reveal the depth of His undying love for you (*Romans 5:8*; *Romans 8:38-39*).

He wants you to experience the abundant life when you allow His love to flow through you (*John 10:10*).

Second, He wants to be your God and Father. He wants you to trust Him like a child should trust a parent. He wants you to experience life knowing your life is in His hands and He will NEVER forsake you, betray you, or stop loving you (*2 Corinthians 6:18*).

Third, He wants to put to death the lies you have believed about yourself and the life lived under that false belief (*Colossians 3:5-10*).

God wants to breathe life into your true identity that was ordained before time (*John 11:25*).

He wants to write your life story with you, with a plot and conclusion that is life-giving and eternal.

What is your response?

If you want to live the life God has designed for you, then pick up your pen and begin to co-write your story with God.

Repent.

Turn from those things that have kept you from living the life God desires and turn toward Jesus (*Psalms 51:1-4*).

Give.

Give all of yourself to Him, including the struggles, the addictions, the pain, and fears. (*Psalms 51:5-7*; *Proverbs 23:26*; *Psalms 73:26*).

Take.

Take on your new identity and new name. Put to death the old self and become new in Christ (*2 Corinthians 5:17*).

Walk.

Walk with the Lord in your true identity, trusting that all that happens is for the good in God who has called you and loves you (*Romans 8:28*; *Galatians 2:20*).

Prayer

Lord, I thank You for creating me with identity and purpose. I reject the false name and identity that I have accepted as truth and have patterned my life.

Jesus, forgive me for making choices according to my will and my justifications. Renew in me a clean heart and create in me a right spirit. Lord I submit all of my life, my name and my identity to You.

Show me who I am to You and lead me on the path you have set for me. I give you my heart and mind. Show me how to walk in the identity and purpose You have ordained for me before time.

Jesus, You are the resurrection and the life. You are the Son of God. Bring life to my true name and purpose. I give you my story, Lord. Make it come true! In Your name, Amen.

Section 2
What is your Talent?

"When I stand before God at the end of my life, I would hope that I would not have a single bit of talent left, and could say, 'I used everything you gave me.'"

—*Erma Bombeck*

Chapter 5
Talents and dreams

What is your talent? For some of us, we can answer this question easily.

I can sing.

I am good at math.

I am a good organizer.

I am good at arts and crafts.

I am a good cook.

It was clear from day one, what we were good at and it was reinforced by those around us who may have praised or invested in our talents.

For others, it may be difficult to answer, especially if we view our lives as a series of failures, unrealized dreams, and unaccomplished goals.

For still others, we struggle with whether we have any talents or gifts at all. We may feel small and insignificant in comparison to "that" person who seems to do it all and have it all. Or others have treated us or told us that we are without talent or distinction…just average.

Talent is defined as the natural endowments of a person:

- a special athletic, creative, or artistic aptitude,

- general intelligence or mental power, or

- ability.

Interestingly, when a talent is mentioned in the Bible it refers to a measure of value. In biblical times, a talent was the largest measure of weight or monetary value. In the Old Testament, one talent weighed about 75 lbs. In the New Testament, a talent was a monetary measure often represented by coins. One talent probably represented up to $30,000 dollars or more in today's currency.

So, whether we understand talent in terms of aptitude and skill or a measure of weight or money, there are a few things common to talents:

1. Talents are made for something. Talents serve a purpose. In a sense, a talent is like a name. It provides identity and in the proper context, even the purpose.

Whitney Houston. Kobe Bryant. Steve Jobs. John Lennon.

When we hear these names, we immediately think about their talent or ability and the impact of these natural talents on society. Even if their lives were marked by tragedy or even scandal, the impact of the negative is still tied to the greatness of their talent or potential.

Whether you consider your abilities and natural aptitude a talent or not, there are things and situations that you are naturally good at doing. You may have applied them to the wrong thing or circumstances, but that which comes easy to you, drives your passion or even angers you may reflect a natural talent and gift that resides inside of you.

2. A talent can be served, given, or exchanged, but by its nature, a talent must be expressed.

How it is expressed depends on the person and the circumstances that exist in that person's life. The same talent it takes to build a successful corporation is the same talent it takes to lead a drug cartel. The same talent it takes to find the best deals, getting more for less, and provide for one's family is the same talent needed for a struggling organization, ministry, or outreach. The same talent it takes to teach or inspire others is the same talent of the most famous inspirational speaker and teacher.

God created you with natural talents and gifts for His purpose. Yet often we do not recognize our own natural gifts and talents, although they are expressed in our daily lives.

One's natural ability may even be perceived as a burden because of what it has brought in your life, seemingly beyond your control.

Another's talent is perceived as common and insignificant, not unique enough to warrant attention or praise.

For some, one's talents and interests may be viewed as weird and quirky, leaving that person feeling inferior, different, and isolated.

Yet, God does not make mistakes. Whether it is the thing you can do without thinking, the unique way you see the world, or how you connect and communicate with others, you are made the way you are and can do what you can do on purpose!

3. Talents bring glory and recognition.

Trees glorify God by their beauty and strength. They also reflect his provision and abundance. The tree trunk is a home for insects, sap for animals, and a hiding place for children at play. The leaves provide food, medicine for the sick, and shade for the laborer. The roots secure and strengthen the soil and bring water from the depth of the earth. Yet the fruit of the tree carries the nourishment for life, whether plucked from the branch or gathered from the ground. The fruit is the food and carries the seed. It is both a blessing and it is life.

Like a tree, your natural abilities and talents are evident in the things or people you protect, nourish, and strengthen in your life. Your purpose is the expressed fruit of your life that brings glory to God and blessings and life to others.

Yet we often take these abilities

and gifts for granted, never considering them as special. Or we use our gifts for vain things that only bring us glory, never experiencing the magnitude of our gifts in God's hands. For it is in God's hands, where we are planted, pruned, and nourished, that we find our purpose—our fruit.

> *¹I am the true grapevine, and my Father is the gardener. ²He cuts off every branch of mine that doesn't produce fruit, and he prunes the branches that do bear fruit so they will produce even more. ³You have already been pruned and purified by the message I have given you. ⁴Remain in me, and I will remain in you. For a branch cannot produce fruit if it is severed from the vine, and you cannot be fruitful unless you remain in me.*
>
> *John 15:1–4*

When you produce much fruit, you are my true disciples. This brings great glory to my Father. John 15:8

²But they delight in the law of the Lord, meditating on it day and night. ³They are like trees planted along the riverbank, bearing fruit each season. Their leaves never wither, and they prosper in all they do. Psalms 1:2–3

Joseph the *Spoiled* Dreamer

Joseph was the eleventh son of Jacob. Jacob had twelve sons in all, from two wives and two concubines. Joseph and his younger brother, Benjamin, were born late in Jacob's life, from his wife Rachel who was also loved more than the other wives.

Like Rebekah, who favored Jacob over his brother, Esau, Jacob loved Joseph above his other children. Jacob went so far as to give Joseph a coat of many colors to wear as a gift of his favor.

This favor caused envy among his older brothers, who hated Joseph for it.

> *Now Israel loved Joseph more than all his children, because he was the son of his old age. Also, he made him a tunic of many colors. But when his brothers saw that their father loved him more than all his brothers, they hated him and could not speak peaceably to him.*
>
> *Genesis 37:3*

Wrath *is* cruel and anger a torrent,
But who *is* able to stand before jealousy?
Proverbs 27:4

Joseph may have made it even easier to be hated by his brothers. Being young and favored, Joseph was a tattler on his brothers and Jacob encouraged this behavior in his son.

Joseph, being seventeen years old, was feeding the flock with his brothers. And the lad was with the sons of Bilhah and the sons of Zilpah, his father's wives; and Joseph brought a bad report of them to his father. Genesis 37:2

> *12Then his brothers went to feed their father's flock in Shechem13AndIsrael said to Joseph, "Are not your brothers feeding the flock in Shechem? Come, I will send you to them."*
>
> *So he said to him, "Here I am."*
>
> *14Then he said to him, "Please go and see if it is well with your brothers and well with the flocks, and bring back word to me." So he sent him out of the Valley of Hebron, and he went to Shechem.*
>
> *Genesis 37:12-14*

Not only is he the favorite young son, he proudly wears his coat of many colors while "checking" on the activities of his older brothers who are much older with families of their own.

Yet, Joseph was more than just an irritating, tattle-telling younger brother with a colorful coat. Joseph was a dreamer, and his dreams would define his life.

> *⁶Now Joseph had a dream, and he told it to his brothers; and they hated him even more. So he said to them, "Please hear this dream which I have dreamed: ⁷There we were, binding sheaves in the field. Then behold, my sheaf arose and also stood upright; and indeed your sheaves stood all around and bowed down to my sheaf."*
>
> *⁸And his brothers said to him, "Shall you indeed reign over us? Or shall you indeed have dominion over us?" So they hated him even more for his dreams and for his words.*
>
> *⁹Then he dreamed still another dream and told it to his brothers, and said, "Look, I have dreamed another dream. And this time, the sun, the moon, and the eleven stars bowed down to me."*
>
> *¹⁰ So he told it to his father and his brothers; and his father rebuked him and said to him, "What is this dream that you have dreamed? Shall your mother and I and your brothers indeed come to bow down to the earth before you?"¹¹ And his brothers envied him, but his father kept the matter in mind.*
>
> *Genesis 37:6-11*

Joseph's dreams were much bigger than his young life could contain. He was not the oldest son who was set to inherit his father's wealth. He was not the strongest son who managed all of the work and labor. He was not even the wisest son, given his lack of sensitivity for his brothers.

Joseph was a young boy and a dreamer.

For us, our dreams are not limited to the nightly adventures we experience in our sleep but can also be the dreams of what we desire our lives to become-the dreams and hopes we have for ourselves. Like Joseph, our dreams may seem too big for our situation or too far-fetched to be realized. Yet, God can speak to us in our dreams and reveal our future in our visions, no matter how unattainable or impossible they may seem.

> [14]*For God speaketh once, yea twice, yet man perceiveth it not.* [15]*In a dream, in a vision of the night, when deep sleep falleth upon men, in slumberings upon the bed;*
>
> [16]*Then he openeth the ears of men, and sealeth their instruction,* [17]*that he may withdraw man from his purpose, and hide pride from man.*
>
> *Job 33:14-17*

And it shall come to pass in the last days, saith God, I will pour out of my Spirit upon all flesh: and your sons and your daughters shall prophesy, and your young men shall see visions, and your old men shall dream dreams. Acts 2:17

Do you think that Joseph or his family understood or believed his dreams?

Do you have dreams or hopes about your life beyond your current reality? If so, what are they? Have you shared your dream or kept it hidden? Why?

The answers to these questions often answer more than just the questions. The answers can provide the reasons why we stop believing or pursuing our dreams.

It may be due to others who have spoken against our dreams, leaving us feeling disheartened and left with self-doubt. Or it might be due to an unexpected and often undesirable event that seemed to close the door on an opportunity to pursue our dreams.

Maybe the dream was too big or too grand to be believed as possible. We often discount our own dreams because we doubt our significance, ability, or worth. Or we battle with the other side of that coin, which is the fear of being exalted or prideful.

What happened to your dream? Does your dream still live inside of you? Have you filed it away as a sweet fantasy of a naïve young girl? Has someone or something killed your dream?

Can you still believe in your dream?

> *"Dreams are illustrations... from the book your soul is writing about you."*
>
> *Marsha Norman 1983 Pulitzer Prize for 'Night Mother,' the Tony Award winner for the Broadway musicals THE SECRET GARDEN and The Color Purple*

A dream near death

Joseph was so hated by his brothers, that they desired to kill him and his dreams. They stripped him of his coat and dropped him in a deep, dry well. While enjoying their lunch, they planned how they might get rid of him for good. A band of Ishmaelites rode by on their way to Egypt. They decided to sell him to the Ishmaelites for 20 pieces of silver.

The brothers took Joseph's colorful coat and dipped it in an animal's blood and brought it to their father. Jacob immediately recognized the coat and assumed a dangerous animal killed his beloved son.

Despite Jacob's inconsolable grief, the brothers allowed him to believe that a wild beast had killed his favored son, Joseph.

> *[34]And Jacob rent his clothes, and put sackcloth upon his loins, and mourned for his son many days. [35]And all his sons and all his daughters rose up to comfort him; but he refused to be comforted; and he said, For I will go down into the grave unto my son mourning. Thus his father wept for him.*
>
> *Genesis 37:34-35*

Prosperity in Poverty

Joseph's life went from bad to worse. He was sold as a slave in the house of the captain of the guard in Egypt – a high-ranking commander in Pharaoh's army named Potiphar. Joseph was now a slave with no family, no coat, living a nightmare...not a dream.

Yet despite his circumstances, God was with Joseph and he prospered even as a slave. Joseph succeeded in everything he did as he served in the home of his Egyptian master. Joseph impressed Potiphar, so he made Joseph his personal attendant. He put him in charge of his entire household and everything he owned.

> *²From the day Joseph was put in charge of his master's household and property, the Lord began to bless Potiphar's household for Joseph's sake. ³All his household affairs ran smoothly, and his crops and livestock flourished. ⁴So Potiphar gave Joseph complete administrative responsibility over everything he owned. With Joseph there, he didn't worry about a thing—except what kind of food to eat!*
>
> *Genesis 39:2-4*

Yet, Joseph's favor was limited. Potiphar's wife found Joseph attractive and relentlessly pressured him to sleep with her. Yet Joseph refused every time, deciding not to betray his master and his God.

> *⁶Joseph was a very handsome and well-built young man, ⁷and Potiphar's wife soon began to look at him lustfully. "Come and sleep with me," she demanded. ⁸But Joseph refused. "Look," he told her, "my master trusts me with everything in his entire household. ⁹No one here has more authority than I do. He has held back nothing from me except you, because you are his wife. How could I do such a wicked thing? It would be a great sin against God." ¹⁰She kept putting pressure on Joseph day after day, but he refused to sleep with her, and he kept out of her way as much as possible.*
>
> *Genesis 39:6-10*

She refused to take no for an answer and trapped him alone in the house. He had no choice but to run away from the temptation, leaving his garment in her hands.

She came and grabbed him by his cloak, demanding, "Come on, sleep with me!" Joseph tore himself away, but he left his cloak in her hand as he ran from the house. Genesis 39:12

Like his colorful coat of many colors, this garment was used against him. Potiphar's wife later presented his garment to the other servants and then to her husband to frame Joseph as a rapist.

> [14]*"Look!" she said. "My husband has brought this Hebrew slave here to make fools of us! He came into my room to rape me, but I screamed.* [15]*When he heard me scream, he ran outside and got away, but he left his cloak behind with me."* [16]*She kept the cloak with her until her husband came home. Then she told him her story. "That Hebrew slave you've brought into our house tried to come in and fool around with me," she said. "But when I screamed, he ran outside, leaving his cloak with me!"*
>
> *Genesis 39:14-16*

Joseph was thrown in jail, no longer a slave but a prisoner. Yet God was with him and he prospered as a prisoner.

> [21]*But the Lord was with Joseph in the prison and showed him his faithful love. And the Lord made Joseph a favorite with the prison warden.* [22]*Before long, the warden put Joseph in charge of all the other prisoners and over everything that happened in the prison.* [23]*The warden had no more worries, because Joseph took care of everything. The Lord was with him and caused everything he did to succeed.*
>
> *Genesis 39:21-23*

Joseph was seventeen when his brothers sold him into slavery and as the years passed, Joseph grew into a man. By no fault of his own, he grew from being a favored son wearing his colorful coat, to becoming a slave and prisoner with no hope of returning home…no family, no father, no coat, and no more dreams.

How often in life, when you are doing the best you can and trying to be the best person you can, that life pulls the rug from under you. Before things get better, it only seems to get worse.

This was Joseph. Joseph was a slave, but he still did the best he could. He remained true to his character, despite his situation. He prospered and all those around him prospered. Yet, when things were as good as they could get, he was falsely accused of rape and placed in prison unjustly.

His dreams were large and big – bigger than the sun, moon, and stars…

"Look, I have dreamed another dream. And this time, the sun, the moon, and the eleven stars bowed down to me." Genesis 37:9

Yet from the moment after he dreamed, his life became smaller. It shrank down to four walls, ankle chains, and a locked prison door.

A dying dream or a dream deferred?

Do you allow yourself to think about what you wanted in your life or to remember the dreams you had for your life, when life looks so much different than what you imagined or dreamed? Life has a way of stealing our dreams away and we can live our lives convinced it was just a dream.

Yet your dream is more than a dream. Even though your life may have turned out different or even the opposite of what you envisioned, your dream is not dead. Moreover, it is very possible, nay, it is *God possible*, that what you have experienced in life, both good and bad, has a purpose and the dream that you dreamed, was too big for the young girl or woman who dreamed it so long ago? Is it possible, that those dreams are meant for the woman you are today?

For today, you are wiser, stronger, experienced, and with more faith than the person of yesteryear.

So, it was for Joseph.

At the beginning of Joseph's story, we know about his dreams, but we knew nothing about his talent or gifts.

By the middle of his story, we see a different Joseph, a gifted Joseph.

>He was a good person.

>He was trustworthy and loyal.

>He was responsible.

>He was a good steward with resources.

>He was a server.

>He was a manager.

>He was a leader.

…and the Lord was with him.

Given all that he went through – envy, hatred, attempted murder, slavery, prison – Joseph could have responded in a number of ways and to most of us, it would have been justified.

Yet he did not respond as most of us might.

>He did not try to escape.

>He did not complain.

He did not attack with anger.

He did not act as a victim.

He did not self-medicate his emptiness or pain.

He honored God no matter what, even when his dreams were shredded and bloodied like his coat of many colors and misrepresented like his slave garment.

Yet, during his years of darkness, Joseph could not have understood how this time was forming him into a person of integrity, strength, and principle. He could not have understood that his dream was not dead…it was waiting.

Can you believe in your dream again, even when your circumstances are so different, dark or hopeless? Can you still believe, when life seems to become harder not easier, and you are doing the best that you can? Can you believe that your dream is still alive and is waiting for you?

Chapter 6
A Talent Discovered

From the Plains to Potiphar to Prison

Joseph's talents were not evident before his trials. Yet they seemed to be formed by the pressure and heat of betrayal, enslavement, and imprisonment.

For many, our talents are obvious, even evident from childhood. (King Solomon was gifted with wisdom from youth.)

For others, our talents are rough and simple, hidden deep below the surface until the pressure and heat of life form them into a talent or a skill. (Moses thought he was the deliverer of Israel because he was a prince of Egypt. Yet he became a criminal and fugitive before his dream would come true.)

For some, the talent is already there, but in a form not recognized as talent. It is not until something erupts and shakes the core of a person that the gem of the talent comes to the surface. (David was only a shepherd boy skilled at fighting large animals to protect his sheep. This bear killer became a giant killer and later, king of Israel.)

For Joseph, he did not create his talents. His dreams were not his making. For it is God that gives us our talents and speaks to us in our dreams about who we are and what we are made for – to serve Him and His plan.

Like Joseph, our dreams and talents do not die just because there is a failure, shame, or loss. Yet, they can be buried beneath the rubble of *what remains.*

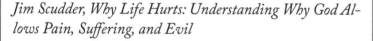
What remains is an appointed time when we are faced with a decision as to how we react and use our talents—to serve God or to serve ourselves.

When Joseph was falsely accused and flung into prison, it was not because he was bad or because he was paying for any wrong done. It was because he needed to be positioned.

Joseph could have easily given up and given in to Potiphar's wife. He was a young handsome man, away from home with no hope for a future. Yet he chose to remain true to his identity and to honor the God of his dreams.

> *"Each day we are becoming a creature of splendid glory or one of unthinkable horror." – Mere Christianity (1952).*

From the Plains to Potiphar to Prison *to the Palace: The Purpose of the Process*

Joseph was never meant to remain in Potiphar's house. He was never meant to remain a slave for what God intended for him. He needed to be positioned closer to his destiny and purpose. He needed to be positioned close to the palace.

While in prison, Joseph prospered. He became the head prisoner and was given responsibility for all the prisoners. Joseph remained there until he was 30 years old, thirteen years from the time he was sold away. It is not hard to imagine his struggle to hold on to hope and a dream for freedom.

Although the Bible does not state if Joseph ever dreamed again, God was not done with Joseph's dreams.

Pharaoh's head butler and baker were thrown into prison for offending the King and Joseph was assigned to these two men. Both men had strange dreams in the same night, which neither could understand.

Joseph offered to interpret their dreams. Joseph told them that in three days the chief butler would be restored to his position, but the chief baker would be beheaded. Both of their dreams came true as Joseph interpreted.

> [12]*"This is what the dream means," Joseph said. "The three branches represent three days.* [13]*Within three days Pharaoh will lift you up and restore you to your position as his chief butler. And please remember me and do me a favor when things go well for you.* [14]*Mention me to Pharaoh, so he might let me out of this place. For I was kidnapped from*

my homeland, the land of the Hebrews, and now I'm here
in prison, but I did nothing to deserve it."

Genesis 40:12-14

For the first time, Joseph shows the cracks of the pressure upon him by telling his story of innocence and pleading to be free in exchange for his favor.

Even with this great favor that Joseph bestowed on the butler (not the baker necessarily), the chief butler forgot about Joseph after he was restored to his position and Joseph was left in prison.

> [20] *Pharaoh's birthday came three days later, and he prepared a banquet for all his officials and staff. He summoned his chief butler and chief baker to join the other officials.* [21] *He then restored the chief butler to his former position, so he could again hand Pharaoh his cup.* [22] *But Pharaoh impaled the chief baker, just as Joseph had predicted when he interpreted his dream.* [23] *Pharaoh's chief butler, however, forgot all about Joseph, never giving him another thought.*

Genesis 40:20-23

Another two years pass by and nothing happens.

Have you ever been at your breaking point, when you cannot take anymore, when there is nothing left to hold on to? How did you respond?

Joseph remains in prison doing the same thing day in and day out, without an answer to the question of how his life ended in such a state. He waited with no hope and no answers until the day Pharaoh has dreams that no one can interpret.

The Pharaoh dreamed two dreams and suddenly Joseph's dreams from long ago began to take breath and come to life.

When there is no one who can interpret the Pharaoh's dreams, the chief butler remembers Joseph and tells Pharaoh of what he did for him in prison.

Suddenly, Joseph was summoned to the palace to interpret the dreams of Pharaoh.

The dreams spoke of seven years of prosperity and abundance in Egypt followed by seven years of famine so severe that the abundance would dry it up as if it never happened (*Genesis 41:29-31*).

Joseph uses his talent and skills and provides a responsible plan to harvest and store food during the time of abundance in order to live during the time of famine (*Genesis 41:33-36*).

Pharaoh trusted Joseph and recognized that God was with Joseph. Like in Jacob's house, Potiphar's house, and the prison house, Joseph was made the highest-ranking official in Egypt, second only to Pharaoh.

> *[39] Then Pharaoh said to Joseph, "Since God has revealed the meaning of the dreams to you, clearly no one else is as intelligent or wise as you are. [40] You will be in charge of my court, and all my people will take orders from you. Only I, sitting on my throne, will have a rank higher than yours."*
>
> *Genesis 41:39-40*

A dream revived.

Joseph's loss and tragedy was more than just random bad luck. It was used to test what was in Joseph. It was used to mold and strengthen under pressure the priceless gem that he was meant to become. His circumstances prepared him for what God intended all along…to make his dreams come true.

Joseph saved Egypt and all the surrounding regions. His brothers sought food from Egypt not knowing that the second in command was, in fact, Joseph.

Before he revealed his identity to his family, Joseph waited until he was sure that his younger brother, Benjamin, was still alive and not victimized as he was. Although it was a dramatic reunion, his brothers were carrying the guilt and shame of what they had done and feared his retaliation. Yet, Joseph was able to look back at all that had occurred and forgave them. He understood that God took what was intended to kill him and his dreams and He turned it into something good…the protection of a family that eventually birthed a nation.

So now it was not you that sent me hither, but God: and he hath made me a father to Pharaoh, and lord of all his house, and a ruler throughout all the land of Egypt. Genesis 45:8

[19]And Joseph said unto them, Fear not: for am I in the place of God? [20]But as for you, ye thought evil against me; but God meant it unto good, to bring to pass, as it is this day, to save much people alive. Genesis 50:19-20

Joseph the Dreamer was the key to the protection and provision of his family and the nation that would come from this family. Though he appeared young and naïve to his family, God knew that He could trust him with his dreams and the path to see those dreams realized.

Likewise, you may feel that you are unimportant with no value or gifts to share, yet God says you are beautiful and wonderfully created. Like Joseph, He trusts you with what He has put in you. Even though the path of life may be dark and seem impossible to repair, God can lead you through that path in order to witness the realization of who you are and what you are created to be.

Like Joseph, you are a key that is meant to unlock the door for others. So, submit the past, the present, and your future to the Lord and He will bring to pass a **perfect good** from the pieces of a tattered and not so perfect life.

Personal Reflection

Back in Time

If you could go back in time and speak to your younger self, are there things you would warn or advise your younger self about? Would you recommend a different decision at a certain point in time? Would you try to convince yourself to say what you needed to say and to whom you needed to say it? Would you tell yourself to listen to that 'voice' inside that told you to stop, to go, to forgive, or to help?

Although you do not have the opportunity to talk to your past self, you have an opportunity to listen to the voice of your future self – the "you" ordained and purposed before creation by God.

You have the opportunity to listen to your future self who sits at the last chapter of your life and who encourages you that it all will "work for the good."

Will you listen to her? Will you believe that your dreams are not dead? Can you remain faithful to the God of your dreams despite the losses and pain? For in His hands, your dreams live and are waiting for the "you" of today.

A Letter from the You of the Last Chapter of Your Life

Dear _____, *(place your name)*

God wants you to trust His plans for you. The dreams you have are not dead. Your talents and skills have been wrought in the fire of your life and are being prepared for great purpose.

So, hold on, don't give up, and don't stop! He never said it was going to be easy. He never said that there would not be trials and persecutions, losses, disease, or death.

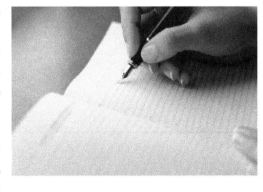

Remember, God is with you in the storm, in the hospital, in the grief, with the betray-al and abuse. Like Joseph, you will survive. You will thrive. You will prosper. Your dreams will come to life if you honor Him with your talent and trust Him with your dreams.

So, press and push for what you cannot see right now. It is there, waiting for you. Do not turn to the right or left. Do not miss out on the great last chapter of your life!

He will provide the miracle!

He will position the promotion!

He will reveal the purpose!

He will restore the sacrifice and the loss!

He will pour to overflow that which has been empty and barren!

Trust and submit to Him that which is most precious and become the diamond you are meant to become.

Love,

_____ *(place your name)*

[1]References

"God, who foresaw your tribulation, has specially armed you to go through it, not without pain but without stain." — *C.S. Lewis*

---

1   2 Thessalonians 1:11-12; Galatians 6:7-; Philippians 3:13-14

Chapter 7
Tested Talents

Talent is the natural endowments of a person. Talent is defined as

- a special athletic, creative, or artistic aptitude,

- general intelligence or mental power, or

- ability.

Often when we think of talents or gifted skills, we think of the positive and admired abilities we see in others. Yet many talents or skills may not be recognized as such, especially if acquired or "molded" under not so positive circumstances.

This is the one who has to lead and bear the burdens of her family even though she never wanted such responsibility, or the one who has the ability to encourage or inspire others but has no one to encourage and lift her up. Even in the context of such contradictions, one's talents and ability may live and breathe.

Rahab was such a contradiction.

Rahab "more than just a prostitute."

In the time of Rahab, the Late Bronze Age, there were three classes of women: (1) slave women, who were the property of the household and performed menial tasks and childcare, (2) citizen women, who owned the slaves and ran the households, and (3) the courtesans, sophisticated companions and prostitutes.

Rahab was in the latter class of women. In such an advanced civilization as Jericho, she may have been considered a woman of great position. Given that her inn was located within the wall of the great city, she was accessible to all traffic in and out of the city and the services she provided were a valued commodity. More than likely, she sold and exchanged more than just sexual favors to wayfarers. Such a woman may have engaged in the import and export of goods, coveted spices and fabrics, thus reaping great wealth and influence in the region.

For a person in her position and reputation, Rahab had to be fiercely independent. She had obvious talents and skills that provided a lifestyle and position that was uncommon for most women of that time or place. She was a successful businesswoman, and she supported her family.

In current times, women hold a record number of successful roles in business, government, science and at home. Yet the skills needed to attain these accomplishments, have often characterized woman as aggressive or proud, unfairly. Yet the journey to these positions in society have been marked by experiences that we may not have personally chosen – "the costs."

One can imagine that Rahab *(Rahab means "proud" and "broad")* may have experienced such a characterization and the 'costs' it demanded.

Rahab was independent and prosperous, with good leadership and a combination of business and street smarts. She was responsible and wise. Although her story is limited to two chapters and two new testament verses, we know from her background and actions, that this woman was no fool!

It was not until she was faced with a decision that would put her and her family at risk, disrupting the very core of her livelihood, that her skills and talents were truly tested.

In her line of work, Rahab had to be current with news, trends, and patterns. Like an investment broker, she had to read the signs of the times and make the best investment with the best return for herself and her family. Facing an impending invasion by the Israelites, she faced the riskiest decision she likely would have to make, to harbor and help the Israeli spies.

She was aware of the rumors concerning the Israelites and their God. She witnessed the fear in the faces and voices of those who frequented her establishment, people in the marketplace, and those in the streets. She knew that the balance of power was shifting and that things would never be the same again.

She took a great risk and bet upon the God of Israel. Yet it was her skills and gifts at determining risk and return, that prepared her to barter for herself and her family.

> *[9b]I know that the Lord has given you the land, that the terror of you has fallen on us, and that all the inhabitants of the land are fainthearted because of you. [10]For we have heard how the Lord dried up the water of the Red Sea for you when you came out of Egypt, and what you did to the two kings of the Amorites who were on the other side of the Jordan, Sihon and Og, whom you utterly destroyed. [11]And as soon as we heard these things, our hearts melted; neither did there remain any more courage in anyone because of you, for the Lord your God, He is God in heaven above and on earth beneath. [12]Now therefore, I beg you, swear to me by the Lord, since I have shown you kindness, that you also will show kindness to my father's house, and give me a true token, and spare my father, my mother, my brothers, my sisters, and all that they have, and deliver our lives from death.*
>
> *Joshua 2:9b–12*

Like Rahab, we have natural gifts and talents that have allowed us to survive in difficult and lean circumstances. Many of us have had to overcome expectations of failure and serve as a source of strength for others. Similarly, Rahab knew how to survive. She invested her talents and skills in an unknown God and a strange people, and it paid off.

While it is true that some gifts are natural and require no effort or practice. More than often, it is the experiences of our lives that molds and sharpens the skills and talents needed to survive and thrive. We may even be ashamed of what we have had to do and how well we do it to survive in life because it is either wrong or looked down upon by friends, family, and even society. Yet, those skills have been forged for survival for ourselves and for those that we love.

Regardless of the source, nothing is wasted in God. This includes the natural talents that come easy and the ones formed by circumstances in our lives that have not been easy.

Furthermore, our gifts and talents often reflect the essence of who we are (identity) and our purpose. However, life may have positioned us in places we never could have imagined. Our lives may not look like anything we dreamed about, yet the dreams, visions, and expectations we had for ourselves are not dead and God has not forgotten them.

There is no story, no matter how tainted or complicated, that God can not include in His story. Yet, there will be a point in your life when you will face the choice of placing all that you have invested, built and value into God's hands. This may come under very difficult times when you are unable to second-guess yourself or question your ability. Like Rahab, this may come when you are facing great sacrifice and risk no matter what action you take.

Yet, like Rahab, when you trust God with all you have and invest it into His hands, the return is life-changing and eternal.

*And Joshua spared **Rahab** the harlot, her father's household, and all that she had. So, she dwells in Israel to this day, because she hid the messengers whom Joshua sent to spy out Jericho. Joshua 6:25*

*By faith the harlot **Rahab** did not perish with those who did not believe, when she had received the spies with peace. Hebrews 11:31*

The curse and the blessing of beauty.

What about those natural traits or talents that place us in positions or categories out of our control? Whether it is a physical feature, a strange sense of humor, or even that condition we may consider more of a defect than a gift, nothing is wasted in God.

This is Esther's story:

Esther was a beautiful young woman who lived in Persia, or present-day Iran. She lived at the time when the Jewish nation, which had been taken away from their land to become slaves, had been allowed to return to Jerusalem where the temple was rebuilt. However, not all Jews returned, and many lived among the regions of Persia under the rule of the Persian King. Esther lived during this time. She and her people lived freely except for following the laws of the land. Esther's parents were deceased and her cousin, Mordecai, who was more like her father, raised her.

It so happens that the king was throwing a three-month-long party to celebrate his kingdom and his riches. On the last day of the celebration, he called for his queen, Vashti, to present herself arrayed in royal dress and wearing her royal crown in order to show off his most prized possession – the Queen. However, the Queen refused to come, and the King and princes of the nation were angry and fearful that all women would learn to disrespect their husbands. So, the king dismissed Vashti as Queen.

The King, needing a wife, ordered all the young and pretty virgins to be brought to the palace. Each young maiden would be summoned to spend time with him. If the king liked her, she would be called back but if not, she would remain a concubine or mistress, and never a queen. After several months of young virgins coming and going, Esther was finally summoned.

Esther presented herself to King Xerxes at the royal palace and he loved Esther more than any of the other young women. He was so delighted with her that he set the royal crown on her head and declared her queen. To celebrate the occasion, he gave a great banquet in Esther's honor for all his nobles and officials, declaring a public holiday for the provinces and giving generous gifts to everyone.

Esther followed Mordecai's directions, just as she did when she lived in his home, and she kept her family background and Jewish nationality a secret (*Esther 2:16-18, 20*).

It is not clear if Esther or Mordecai viewed these circumstances as a curse or a blessing. A blessing, since now Esther lived a life of luxury with servants of her own. A curse, since she was separated from her family and people and under the complete control of the king who could do with her as he chose.

Do you have a physical feature or personality trait that impacts how you are perceived or treated, for good or bad?

Regardless of how Esther or Mordecai perceived the situation, it is likely that Esther really had no idea what her future would hold. Yet God was already working things out for her and the nation of Israel.

How Esther chose to respond would have a direct impact on her life and those close to her.

"Life is a tapestry: We are the warp; angels, the weft; God, the weaver. Only the Weaver sees the whole design."

– Eileen Elias Freeman

The Grand Weaver

The journey of life is made up of times, seasons, transitions, losses, and gains, yet God has purposed every part for His will.

¹To everything there is a season and a time to every purpose under the heaven: ²A time to be born, and a time to die; a time to plant, and a time to pluck up that which is planted; ³A time to kill, and a time to heal; a time to break down, and a time to build up; ⁴A time to weep, and a time to laugh; a time to mourn, and a time to dance; ⁵A time to cast away stones, and a time to gather stones together; a time to embrace, and a time to refrain from embracing; ⁶A time to get, and a time to lose; a time to keep, and a time to cast away; ⁷A time to rend, and a time to sew; a time to keep silence, and a time to speak; ⁸A time to love, and a time to hate; a time of war, and a time of peace.

Ecclesiastes 3:1-8

We live in moments that are tied together by one event to the next. Yet we lack the overview of our journey and the "times and seasons" it contains. We cannot make sense of the order or connection of things or events. Yet, He sees our lives from the end to the beginning and weaves it into His greater will and plan.

⁹Remember the former things of old; for I am God and there is none else; I am God, and there is none like me, ¹⁰Declaring the end from the beginning, and from ancient times the things that are not yet done, saying, "My counsel shall stand, and I will do all my pleasure."

Isaiah 46:9-10

Our journey of life, with all of its twists and turns, may not make sense to us, but God sees the connection. When we place our lives – all of it – in His hand, He connects the seasons of our lives in a way that works for our good. Even the losses are connected to other events that can catapult us to the next level and opportunity.

And we know that all things work together for good to them that love God, to them who are the called according to his purpose. Romans 8:28

So, it was with the interwoven story of Mordecai, Esther, and the Hebrew people.

The Threads

When you do something good that seems to go unnoticed or unrewarded.

> Mordecai overhears two of the king's servants plotting to kill him and he's able to get a message to Esther, saving the king's life. Yet Mordecai is not recognized, but a record of this is kept in the King's book (*Esther 2:21-23*).

When the one you love is taken away or abandons you due to circumstance out of your control and you have no way to protect them or get them back.

> Esther is taken from Mordecai to become the wife of the king. Mordecai has limited access and influence on her safety, wellbeing, and lifestyle (*Esther Chapter 2*).

When you are obedient to God's commands and do what is right and it results in trials and tribulations for you and those you love.

> Haman, a prince of Persia and second in command to the king, is offended at Mordecai for not kneeling and worshipping him. He then sets forth a plan. He speaks to the king who approves of his plan to kill all the Jews and to take all of their wealth and put it in the king's treasury (*Esther 3:1-15*).

You are suffering and distressed yet no one seems to understand the depth of your distress and pain.

> The Jews and Mordecai panic and grieve out of fear about what is to take place. Esther tries to comfort her cousin with new clothes, yet he will not accept them (*Esther 4:1-3*).

At a point of breaking, you must decide to place your faith in God and His plan even with fear of great loss.

> Mordecai instructs Esther to speak with the king and request that he stop this plan. He must depend on Esther to take the risk of going to the king with this request, placing herself and the Jewish people in imminent danger of death.
>
> Esther is afraid but after prayer and fasting goes to the king who favors her for her natural gifts...her beauty and gentleness.

God is moving behind the scenes not only for His will but also for your good because of your obedience and trust in His will and His provision.

> Esther is unaware that other events are occurring that will intersect with her actions at just the right time.
>
> Haman creates gallows to hang Mordecai as he prepares to be honored by the King.
>
> The king rises from a sleepless night and decides to read the record of Mordecai's message that saved his life. The king wants to honor this man, not aware he is the target of Haman's hatred.
>
> Thinking it is for himself, Haman proposes a great celebration to honor this man who has saved the king, but then has to witnesses his glory bestowed upon Mordecai.
>
> Esther reveals to the King the evil plan of Haman against herself and her people. The King then hangs Haman upon the very gallows he had built for Mordecai. Mordecai is placed second in command to the King and Esther remains as the celebrated Queen (*Esther Chapters 4-10*).

To Mordecai, Esther, and all others, these events were separate events, each with its own sets of challenges and choices. It is unlikely that Mordecai was aware that his good deed of saving the king from assassination would one day be revealed to the King at just the right time.

Esther had no idea that her enslavement in a forced marriage, away from family and culture, would actually position her close to the King's heart and ear to intercede for her people.

Haman had no idea that his original plan to annihilate Mordecai and the Jewish nation would actually be the plan for his own demise and destruction.

God took:

1) a good deed that went unnoticed;
2) a loved one taken from her family and people;
3) an injustice against an innocent man and nation; and
4) **one act of faith from an unassuming young girl,**

and weaves a story that results in:

1) a faithful servant who is glorified before his enemies;
2) the security and blessing for a young woman, her uncle, and her family;
3) the righteous judgment of an enemy; and
4) **the deliverance of a people and nation.**

God knows the times and seasons of the individual, the family, the community, and the nation. He knows the past stories, the current stories, and the future stories, and in His great wisdom and love, creates a story that ends with beauty, salvation, and His glory.

The key to our story becoming a part of God's story is the choice we make at that crossroads in our lives, when we must choose to give all of ourselves and what we value to God, or not.

Since God is sovereign, His ultimate will and plan will be accomplished whether we choose Him or not. Yet God has chosen us right where we are in our lives, no matter the situation or circumstance, to make that choice. His story is made up of your story and He wants to make it a glorious one of redemption, renewal, and deliverance.

Bookmark: Made for a Day

Festival of Purim is a Jewish holiday that occurs in 12th month of the Hebrew Calendar. It commemorates the day that the Persian King revoked the decree to destroy the Jews. It is a celebration of the Jewish nation triumphing over its enemies in Persia. Esther's story is read a loud and she is cheered whenever her name is called. It is day of great celebration and festivity.

 However, there is another important day linked to this story of victory that begs a question.

When Esther went before the King unannounced to advocate for her people, the people were instructed to fast and pray for three days before she made her plea before the king. This time of intercession and redemption occurred one month before another consecrated day, Passover. Jesus was sacrificed as our Passover lamb and was resurrected three days later with victory. Likewise, three days after a call of fasting and praying, Esther went before the King seeking salvation and redemption.

For Esther, Mordecai, you and I, Christ shows us there is a link between sacrifice, and redemption . There is an appointed day when we must choose whether to sacrifice our gifts, our talents, and ourselves. Like Christ, Esther was created and uniquely made for this point in time. Her beauty was not her choosing but it was a gift that positioned her for sacrifice and subsequent victory.

In. the end, Esther did not know that her life, her beauty, and her sacrifice would be celebrated as the day of Purim for ages to come.

You too, are also made for a 'day.' How will you respond?

Such A Time as This

Mordecai sent this reply to Esther, "Don't think for a moment that because you're in the palace you will escape when all other Jews are killed. If you keep quiet at a time like this, deliverance and relief for the Jews will arise from some other place, but you and your relatives will die. *Who knows if perhaps you were made queen for just such a time as this?*"

Like Esther and Rahab, you are made for this time, this season, and this circumstance.

Your gifts and talents and the value they have brought to your life were designed for a purpose and a time that God has ordained. How we use those gifts and talents, determines the impact upon our lives, but also the lives of our family, community and potentially generations to come.

Like Esther, like Joseph, and like Rahab, don't allow yourself to be distracted by the "parts" and the "players" of your story. Trust that God has the plot of your story, and the plot of everyone else's story, already completed. Choose to honor God with who He ordained you be and what He equipped you to do, no matter if you can see or predict the outcome. It is His will to use you, not for your loss but for your gain. Trust that the outcome will be good; good for you and good for others in the end.

"For I know the plans I have for you," says the Lord. "They are plans for good and not for disaster, to give you a future and a hope." Jeremiah 29:11

⁹Salvation is not a reward for the good things we have done, so none of us can boast about it. ¹⁰For we are God's masterpiece. He has created us anew in Christ Jesus, so we can do the good things he planned for us long ago. Ephesians 2:9-10

Personal Reflection

When we are facing a God-ordained crossroad, how should we respond? How do we walk in the will of God, investing our talents and gifts in His will and not of our own?

1)   Do not lean on your own understanding.

Trust in the Lord with all your heart; do not depend on your own understanding. Proverbs 3:5

2)   Agree with God, trusting Him by His word.

But Jesus told him, "No! The Scriptures say, 'People do not live by bread alone, but by every word that comes from the mouth of God.'" Matthew 4:4

3)   Obey Him even when it feels like He is silent or far away.

> But Samuel replied, "What is more pleasing to the Lord:
>
> your burnt offerings and sacrifices or your obedience to his voice? Listen! Obedience is better than sacrifice, and submission is better than offering the fat of rams."
>
> 1 Samuel 15:22

4)   Trust God with how He made you, where He placed you, and with what He gifted you (*Exodus 4:11*; *Jeremiah 1:4-18*).

The Lord asked him, "Who gave humans their mouths? Who makes humans unable to talk or hear? Who gives them sight or makes them blind? It is I, the Lord! Now go, and I will help you speak and will teach you what to say." Exodus 4:11

Before I formed you in the womb I knew you; Before you were born I sanctified you; I ordained you a prophet to the nations. Jeremiah 1:4

Prayer

Lord, Jesus, thank You for how you made me. Thank You for my talents, my quirks, and my sensibilities. Lord, I even thank You for those things I have considered handicaps or burdens. I praise You for I am fearfully and wonderfully made!

Lord forgive me for using my gifts and talents, my strengths, for my glory and my promotion. Forgive me when I left others by the wayside, cut corners, or cheated to get ahead and ensure my own survival. I repent and turn from the selfish choices I have made.

Lord, thank You for my dreams. Thank You for the hope I carried so long ago. I pray that You breathe life to the dreams and gifts You placed inside me. Teach me Your ways and lead me in Your way everlasting. Abide in me as I abide in You and let the fruit of my life be to Your glory.

I place it all on Your altar and give it back to You. Take it and use it according to Your will. Teach me to wait upon You, Lord. Give me strength to stand upon Your promises. Show me how to be still and to know that You, and You alone, are God. In your name, Jesus. Amen

Section 3
What is in your heart?

I will give you a new heart and put a new spirit within you; I will take the heart of stone out of your flesh and give you a heart of flesh.

Ezekiel 36:26

Chapter 8
Love, Gifts, Sacrifices

What is love to you? What comes to your mind? Is it a flutter in your chest, sweaty palms, a warm fuzzy, or a feeling of overwhelming desire?

If you ask different people, the answers may vary widely. Even if you ask the same person, the answer may change depending on their age, day, or mood of that person.

In fact, how we define love often comes from our own experiences with what we call "love." For one person, love is seen as controlling, angry, and distrustful. For another, love is provision and support. Still, for some, love is like a drug that brings the high of excitement and desire and the lows of detachment and disappointment.

What about those who do not believe in love, have never been loved, or have been failed by love?

However, we identify love, most of us would agree that there are different types of love.

In the English language, many definitions of "love" exist. Merriam Webster's dictionary provides several[2]:

> (1) Strong affection for another arising out of kinship or personal ties maternal *love* for a child

> (2) Attraction based on sexual desire: affection and tenderness felt by lovers

> (3) Affection based on admiration, benevolence, or common interests *love* for his old schoolmates

---

2 https://www.merriam-webster.com/dictionary/love

(4) Unselfish loyal and benevolent concern for the good of another: such as (a) the fatherly concern of God for humankind (b) brotherly concern for others

(5) An amorous episode: love affair

(6) The sexual embrace: copulation

Love /ἀγάπη/

In the Greek[3], the language of the New Testament, there are also different words for love reflecting different kinds of *love*.

Agápe – charity; the love of God for man and of man for God; the unconditional love of God for his children. This type of love was further explained as "to will the good of another."

Eros – "love, mostly of the sexual passion." Appreciation of the beauty within that person, or even becomes an appreciation of beauty itself.

Philía – means "affectionate regard, friendship," usually "be-tween equals." Aristotle described it as loyalty to friends (specifically, "brotherly love"), family, and community, and requires virtue, equality, and familiarity.

Storgē – "love, affection"; common or natural empathy; the love for one's country or a favorite sports team.

So, there are many definitions of love, used for different relationships and situations. These definitions describe the myriad of emotions, decisions, and actions for which love is held responsible. However, such variety can also breed confusion especially when people have different views of love and how it applies to their respective relationships.

A young woman may feel that she is falling in love with her boyfriend with all the bells and whistles of romance and passion sounding off in her heart, i.e., *Eros or passionate love*. Whereas the man cares and enjoys the relationship with the woman yet views it as more of a friendly kind of love, i.e. *Philia or platonic love* – a common scenario that un-

---

3   https://en.wikipedia.org/wiki/Greek_words_for_love

fortunately leads to confusion and heartbreak.

How often are we caught up in confusing, possibly hurtful, situations because of the various expressions of what is defined as *love* today?

Can "love" really have one definition or meaning?

Love

 If we go to the language of the Old Testament, the word "love," has one single meaning. Love in Hebrew is "Ahava," which is made up of three basic Hebrew letters. These three letters actually are broken down into two parts: a two-letter base or root, and the first letter, which is a modifier. The meaning of the two-letter base is "to give." The letter "aleph," which precedes these two letters comes to modify the meaning of the base word, "give." Thus, the meaning of "Ahava" or "love" is "*I give.*"

In distinct contrast to ancient and modern languages, ancient and Modern Hebrew has one single word for love with one definition – I give. It is not a feeling word. It is an action word.

In the Old Testament, when love is written, only this Hebrew word is used. Whether it is expressed between God and man, man to God, or man to man (woman or child), love has one definition, and it is to give.

How do you define giving? How do you relate giving to loving?

What if you give and do not get in return that which you need, expect, or desire?

Yet, even the act of giving can be qualified and characterized by different emotions or motives, such as guilt, obligation, charity, sympathy, or recognition.

In fact, if we are honest, there are times that even when we give charitably, there may be an unexpressed expectation of return. Whether it is our time, money, or commitment, we crave or expect some return for our sacrifice.

These feelings are not necessarily sinful, for even when we give unconditionally, there is the "reward" of knowing that we gave unconditionally.

However, sin can emerge, when there is a sense of entitlement or expectation of return for the sacrifice. If we do not receive it, it can taint our ability to give again.

"I bought him the watch he has been wanting, and he still ignores me for Facebook and fantasy football."

"I manage all of Daddy's care. I was up three times last night, changing the bed and his bedclothes. Do you think any of my brothers and sisters have even offered to give me a break or ask if I need some support?"

"I have served as an usher for five years, barely missing a Sunday. She just joined the church a year ago and they have assigned her to be over counting the money."

"I am not going to volunteer on that committee anymore. They need to ask for more volunteers. After all these years of serving and they are just now giving me a recognition pin."

This is not to say that when we feel we are being taken for granted, ignored, or not recognized, that we are not justified in our expectations for recognition or our feelings of offense. There is a natural and spiritual law of giving and receiving, sowing and reaping, and God has promised that if we give there shall be a receiving, proportionately.

Give, and it will be given to you: good measure, pressed down, shaken to-

gether, and running over will be put into your bosom. For with the same measure that you use, it will be measured back to you. Luke 6:38

But this I say: "He who sows sparingly will also reap sparingly, and he who sows bountifully will also reap bountifully." 2 Corinthians 9:6

Yet the giving or loving, that God requires of us, does not require justification, recognition, or reward.

So let each one give as he purposes in his heart, not grudgingly or of necessity; for God loves a cheerful giver. 2 Corinthians 9:7

> [1]*Take heed that you do not do your charitable deeds before men, to be seen by them. Otherwise you have no reward from your Father in heaven. [2]Therefore, when you do a charitable deed, do not sound a trumpet before you as the hypocrites do in the synagogues and in the streets, that they may have glory from men. Assuredly, I say to you, they have their reward. [3]But when you do a charitable deed, do not let your left hand know what your right hand is doing, [4]that your charitable deed may be in secret; and your Father who sees in secret will Himself reward you openly.*
>
> *Matthew 6:1-4*

Actually, giving in the kingdom of God is equated to sacrifice.

Sacrifice is defined as:

- An act of offering to a deity something precious; especially, the killing of a victim on an altar, or

- Destruction or surrender of something for the sake of something else, or

- Something given up or lost, usually for the sake of a better cause i.e., the sacrifices made by parents.

The sacrifices of the Old Testament were to be of one's free will, the first and best of your resources and possessions. It was to be without defect or disease, i.e., pure.

And whoever offers a sacrifice of a peace offering to the Lord, to fulfill his vow, or a freewill offering from the cattle or the sheep, it must be perfect to be accepted; there shall be no defect in it. Leviticus 22:21

And when you offer a sacrifice of thanksgiving to the Lord, offer it of your own free will. Leviticus 22:29

The significance of the sacrifice was that it required the giver to give away something valuable, desired, and personal. The sacrifice was to be given without a measurable return or at a great loss to the person.

Have you ever had to sacrifice something valuable or "at a loss to you" for someone else? How did you feel about it and why?

How about the sacrifice of an apology or saying, "I am sorry," when your pride tells you to remain angry or defensive?

How we sacrifice or give, is a reflection of how we feel about the person we are sacrificing to. It also reflects how we view ourselves in relation to the recipient. In fact, to God, true sacrifice is without regret, resentment, or disregard. It is done generously and openly. It is not tainted by self-gain, self-recognition, or self-promotion. It is **pure**.

King David was a blessed king, anointed as a boy, a killer of giants, and a leader of a nation. Yet David sinned greatly. He took another man's wife, slept with her, and impregnated her. The husband was one of his chief military officers who honored and trusted David, but David felt justified to "cover" his tracks and arranged for her husband to be killed. He married the widow (which on the surface was legal under God's law) so no one would discover his sin.

The prophet of God confronted David with the truth of his sin and declared God's judgment against David and his family.

David did not respond with a list of reasons why it happened, nor did he displace blame. He did not tell the prophet "she seduced me or trapped me," or "I'm just a man, I couldn't help it," or "God has already let me have many wives, widows, and concubines and I have never heard a word about this before."

His response to the man of God was:

So David said to Nathan, "I have sinned against the Lord."

2 Samuel 12:13a

His response to God was:

> *[1]Have mercy upon me, O God,*
>
> *According to Your lovingkindness;*
>
> *According to the multitude of Your tender mercies,*
>
> *Blot out my transgressions.*
>
> *[2]Wash me thoroughly from my iniquity,*

And cleanse me from my sin.

³For I acknowledge my transgressions,

And my sin is always before me.

⁴Against You, You only, have I sinned,

And done this evil in Your sight—

That You may be found just when You speak,

And blameless when You judge.

Psalm 51:1-4

David could have just put a sin offering on the altar of the temple, which was lawful and right under the law. He could have only expressed his admission to his pastor or friend and waited for God's punishment. Instead, he sacrificed repentance directly unto God. David sacrificed his pride and position because he ultimately valued God over himself.

This is true sacrifice. This is true giving. This is true love. True love is giving to God selflessly, not thinking of our self, but trusting His ways and judgments, even in repentance.

In fact, because of David's response, God honored his sacrifice and had mercy on him, sparing his life (and his destiny) although God's judgment was completed.

¹³ᵇAnd Nathan said to David, "The Lord also has put away your sin; you shall not die. ¹⁴However, because by this deed you have given great occasion to the enemies of the Lord to blaspheme, the child also who is born to you shall surely die." 2 Samuel 12:13b-14

Such sacrifice of love may be easier to accept (although not always easier to do) when directed to God in obedience, worship, or repentance.

What are the challenges when we are confronted to love those who have wronged us, those who are different than us, or when it is just inconvenient to do so?

Some of the challenges we face in loving or sacrificing for others are related to issues of unforgiveness, fear, distrust, pride, or shame. Actually, we can name many challenges or issues that affect our ability to love others as God loves us. Yet, if we look at all of our challenges, there exists a common theme to them, SIN. All of the possible issues that prevent us from fully loving others are due to sin. Fear comes from not trusting, which is sin. Unforgiveness comes from pride, which is sin. Pride and shame are fed by fear, which is sin. (Vicious cycle, right?)

Again, the central theme of all of these challenges is *SIN*.

Self. Indulging. Need.

Every expressed sin first started with a decision to 'feed' or nurture self even at the expense of the 'hungry' souls around us.

I can't forgive that.

I will never trust him again.

I don't deal with those people.

I have too many things to do.

She was never there for *me*.

I deserve better than this.

I do not love him anymore.

They never liked *me*.

You never listen to *me*.

I can only take so much of him.

They are so strange…*I* can't *even* deal.

Why do *I* always have to do it?

When is it going to be *my* turn?

We can't associate with them. They don't believe like *we* do.

Anything that places our attention, love, and investment on "self" at the expense of others will always be associated with sin—whether hidden in one's heart or displayed in our actions.

True sacrifice actually requires giving pieces of yourself away to edify or nourish someone else at your expense, even if they reject your offering.

Therefore, it is impossible to love others sacrificially, when these "challenges" remain. Moreover, the "challenges" or issues of our hearts prevent us from loving or giving unto God sacrificially, as well.

Although we may believe we love God, if our heart toward others is tainted by judgment, revenge, bitterness, distrust, or prejudice than we are giving God the same, for what flows between us and God automatically flows from us to others.

> "True love germinates in the soil of sacrifice, sprouts in the garden of surrender, and matures in a matrimony of servant hood. Love isn't love until it has cost you something to give it away."
>
> —Kris Vallotton Source/Notes: Purity: The New Moral Revolution (2008), p. 55

To the pure all things are pure, but to those who are defiled and unbelieving nothing is pure; but even their mind and conscience are defiled. Titus 1:15.

In fact, one can judge a person's relationship with God based on their relationship with those "near" to them. If we *love* selfishly or conditionally, then we approach God the same way. If we love unconditionally, fully, and consistently, then we love God the same way, even when life disappoints.

> *[19] We love because he first loved us. If anyone says, "I love God," and hates his brother, he is a liar; [20] for he who does not love his brother whom he has seen cannot love God whom he has not seen. [21] And this commandment we have*

from him: whoever loves God must also love his brother.

1 John 14:19–21

⁷Beloved let us love one another, for love is from God, and whoever loves has been born of God and knows God. ⁸Anyone who does not love does not know God, because God is love. 1 John 4:7–8

Personal Reflection

By answering these questions honestly, we can begin to peel back the barriers to the "sacrificial" love we are to give.

Do I give love unconditionally, even when I am not guaranteed a return of that love?

If not, what keeps me from loving unconditionally?

How do I set boundaries and still love as God commands?

Some may question how much to sacrifice or love others, yet successfully set boundaries. Do we give even at the expense of our values, morals, and righteousness?

The answer is no. God would never expect you to compromise what is right in His eyes in order to sacrifice to others, as that cancels out our first love for Him.

Even Jesus told Peter to "get behind me" and called Peter's selfish desire as "satan" because it rejected Christ's passion and purpose; a purpose that is the complete expression of God's love for all humanity (*Matthew 16:21–24*).

What would be the result if you loved God and others as God commands?

God does not require us to keep these commands for his own satisfaction or ego. These commands to love are so powerful that if we commit ourselves to truly loving and giving all to Christ, then it allows Him to pour His love in us. From there we can pour out His love to others. It is not about giving it away in vain but about receiving it as overflow and giving it away to those who are spiritually poor and devoid of His love and redemption.

In the end, God uses us to love others to Christ. In the process of loving or giving sacrificially, we are healed and made whole by the giving...the *Ahava*.

> "It is not enough for us to say, 'I love God, but I do not love my neighbor, since in dying on the Cross, God had [made] himself the hungry one – the naked one – the homeless one... Jesus' hunger,' she said, 'is what you and I must find and alleviate.'"
>
> Mother Theresa, Nobel Prize Acceptance Speech December 11, 1970

Chapter 9
A Heart Condition

And you must love the Lord your God with all your heart, all your soul, and all your strength. Deuteronomy 11:1

And now, Israel, what does the Lord your God require of you? He requires only that you fear the Lord your God, and live in a way that pleases him, and love him and serve him with all your heart and soul. Deuteronomy 10:12

But be very careful to obey all the commands and the instructions that Moses gave to you. Love the Lord your God, walk in all his ways, obey his commands, hold firmly to him, and serve him with all your heart and all your soul. Joshua 22:5

So be very careful to love the Lord your God. Joshua 23:11

The Bible is full of verses that command and caution us to love and sacrifice all to God as the Lord of our lives – heart, soul, and strength. This means no walls, blocks, or defenses. We relinquish our rights, our selves, and our interests to that of God. We choose Him and what He wants over what we desire, want, or think.

The truth is many do not know what that really means, much less how to accomplish such sacrifice. The competition of our needs, desires, and opinions for preeminence in our lives is a continuous battle that we may lose even before we are aware that we have lost.

It is not a matter of whether we believe or even love God. The problem is we struggle with placing His value above our own, whether we are aware of it or not.

It is easy to reject this statement as it may offend how you view your relationship with God. You may even feel it is unfairly judgmental. Yet, anything we consider of great value will be reflected in our actions toward it. For the depth and quality of love is measured by the perceived intrinsic value of the person or thing loved. The question is, who or what do you most value?

> [19]*Lay not up for yourselves treasures upon earth, where moth and rust doth corrupt, and where thieves break through and steal:*
>
> [20]*But lay up for yourselves treasures in heaven, where neither moth nor rust doth corrupt, and where thieves do not break through nor steal:* [21]*For where your treasure is, there will your heart be also.*
>
> *Matthew 6:19-21*

We will sacrifice our time, money, bodies, gifts, and even our own welfare for things or people that we consider highly valuable.

Have you ever done something at great sacrifice to yourself, because it was for someone you cared about or loved?

Why?

In fact, if you wonder who or what you love the most, follow the "trail" of sacrifices you have made in your life. Whoever or whatever has the longest and widest trail, is the object of your deepest love.

Who or what in your life has the longest trail of sacrifices?

How does your "trail" of sacrifices to God line up in comparison?

Of course, love for others is a good thing since we are also commanded to love others as we love ourselves.

> [30]And thou shalt love the Lord thy God with all thy heart, and with all thy soul, and with all thy mind, and with all thy strength: this is the first commandment. [31]And the second is like, namely this, Thou shalt love thy neighbor as thyself. There is none other commandment greater than these.
>
> Mark 12:30-31

We can do this more easily for those closest and dearest to us. Yet, for some this task may be harder to do when faced with loving and sacrificing for those who are outside of our inner circle or close friends and family.

Have you ever made a quick judgment of someone based on their dress, race, gender, state of being, or even their past mistakes?

Have you ever held a grudge for an injustice or betrayal and allowed those feelings to prevent you from showing love and forgiveness when the opportunity presented itself?

Have you ever said no to someone who needed your help because you judged them unworthy or because they refused to help you in your time of need?

When was the last time you reacted or overreacted badly to something someone said or did, because you believed they were being disrespectful, cheating, or taking advantage of you?

If we are honest, we would have to answer "yes" to most of these scenarios. In fact, when we look back at our lives, we may recognize those moments that need to be repented of, because we chose our interests, needs, and desires over someone else's, even when it cost us little to sacrifice. This is especially true for those we do not consider as close loved ones.

Yet we may even struggle with those with whom we hold dear. We may still find ourselves struggling with impulses of anger, frustration, distrust, excessive criticism, withdrawal, selfishness, or impatience. Furthermore, we may tend to behave in these ways in certain situations or in response to certain behaviors.

"I am not going to tell her about the new job opening. She acts like she's everyone's boss anyway."

"I have nothing to say. He's not going to talk to me, then I'm not going to say anything either. If he wants to leave, then fine. I don't need him anyway."

"I'll say, 'I'm sorry,' when she says she's sorry."

"No. I don't think I will invite her. You know, she didn't invite us to her ceremony – some crazy lie about wanting a small ceremony just for her immediate family."

"I had an affair because there was nothing left after all these years. He ignored me, criticized me, and treated me like a door mat…so when Matt came along…I just got swept away in the passion. I couldn't help it."

"After all that I've done and sacrificed, I still haven't received the raise I deserve. They owe me this cash. Shoot, they won't miss this little bit, anyway."

In the world, we have labeled these behaviors as "issues." We have issues with men, issues with supervisors and co-workers, issues with family, issues with trust, issues with money. Yet our "issues" are a direct reflection of the condition of our heart. Our heart is the most vulnerable part of ourselves from which flows all that is good and bad within us. How we perceive, react, and act can be tied to what is in our hearts.

Keep thy heart with all diligence; for out of it are the issues of life. Proverbs 4:23

What is in your heart? What are your issues?

Do you still struggle with loving others or God as the Bible commands?

Why do you think it is difficult at times to love others or even God as it is commanded?

"Oh, wretched woman that I am!"

We all struggle with the "disconnect" of what is required of our Christian lives and what we are capable of achieving. The fact is, we are incapable of loving like God, without God. As spirit-filled believers, we may still have significant struggles with anger, anxiety, and fear. This can disrupt our ability to vulnerably connect with people making it impossible to love them sacrificially as God commands.

Often, we "give up" with a hopeless acceptance that "This is just the way I am," or the declaration that, "God's not finished with me yet," or "Sorry, that's just not me." Or we change our understanding of what is commanded of us to, "I don't believe God really expects me to do that. It is not that literal."

These sentiments do not necessarily reflect an intent to reject the commandment to love but may reflect the human condition from which every human suffers. The truth is we all struggle with loving others and God. This struggle is expected as we are wrapped in sinful flesh.

> *[18]For I know that in me (that is, in my flesh,) dwelleth no good thing: for to will is present with me; but how to perform that which is good I find not. [19]For the good that I*

would I do not: but the evil which I would not, that I do.
²⁰Now if I do that I would not, it is no more I that do it, but
sin that dwelleth in me.

²¹I find then a law, that, when I would do good, evil is
present with me. ²²For I delight in the law of God after
the inward man: ²³But I see another law in my members,
warring against the law of my mind, and bringing me into
captivity to the law of sin which is in my members. ²⁴O
wretched man that I am! who shall deliver me from the
body of this death?

Romans 7:18-24

It becomes an issue when we remain stagnant in our Christian walk and continually battle the same struggles or repeat the same mistakes, wondering why we remain the same and never grow beyond these issues.

¹Brothers and sisters, I could not address you as people
who live by the Spirit but as people who are still world-
ly—mere infants in Christ. ²I gave you milk, not solid food,
for you were not yet ready for it. Indeed, you are still not
ready. ³You are still worldly. For since there is jealousy and
quarreling among you, are you not worldly? Are you not
acting like mere humans?

1 Corinthians 3:1-3

This can be especially disheartening when the word of God tells us that if we are in Christ, we are new creatures. Or, if we have crucified the flesh, we will show the fruits of the spirit, of which love is primary, thus fulfilling the whole law.

Therefore, if anyone is in Christ, he is a new creation; old things have passed away; behold, all things have become new. 2 Corinthians 5:17

²²But the fruit of the Spirit is love, joy, peace, patience, kindness, goodness, faith, ²³gentleness, self-control. Against such things there is no law. ²⁴Now those who belong to Christ Jesus have crucified the flesh with its passions and desires. Galatians 5:22-24

For the whole law is fulfilled in one word: "You shall love your neighbor as yourself." Galatians 5:14

Yet, because we are wrapped in a sinful body that desires to please and satisfy itself first, we must identify those issues that prevent us from learning how to love God and love others as ourselves in all of our relationships. For the Greek word used for love in the Bible verse in Galatians Chapter 5 is *agape* – the unconditional, sacrificial love independent of the type of relationship or the persons in the relationship.

> *⁷Beloved, let us love* [agape] *one another, for love* [agape] *is from God, and whoever loves* [agape] *has been born of God and knows God.*
>
> *⁸Anyone who does not love* [agape] *does not know God, because God is love* [agape].
>
> *1 John 4:7-8*

Can you recognize any issues, behaviors, or attitudes that continue to negatively impact your relationships?

How does it make you feel about yourself?

How does it make you feel about God and His view of you?

Answering such questions may leave some of us feeling unworthy, ashamed, defensive, or condemned because such struggles still persist in our lives despite our best efforts.

Why do we still struggle? Is it because we are just weak, uncommitted Christians who haven't done enough for God? Is it because God has granted others more power than us to live a better Christian life? Is it because of our sin that has not been crucified?

The answer to these questions may be more complicated than a yes or no answer.

It is true that unforgiveness, selfishness, pride, greed, lust, and rebellion are all sins that directly prevent us from growing in faith, obedience, and love.

Yet, there is an underlying condition of our hearts that exists before sin even raises its ugly head. It is this condition that God has been trying to address since He created us.

Since before time, God understood what this condition is and the destruction it would have on the one thing for which we were created do which is to love Him and be loved by Him.

It's not about sin. It's about shame.

> *"Why had no one protected her? By the time she was 26yrs old she had slept with over 15 men and endured two abortions. But the sex began when she was eleven, with an uncle who had first treated her as special but eventually threatened her life if she were to reveal the horror. This lasted until she was seventeen, when she left for college, where she was free of her uncle but imprisoned to the behavior that was the only path she knew to intimacy with a man. How in the world was she to tell her parents, let alone her friends or anyone in her faith community? The only reason she was telling me was that her depression had become too overwhelming for her to function."* – excerpt from The Soul of Shame by Curt Thompson, MD

Shame is something that everyone has experienced, whether it is the embarrassment inflicted by a teasing friend or the shame we carry from our mistakes and failings. No matter one's story or their background, we are all plagued with shame.

Shame is hard to define. Some may call it humiliation, embarrassment, or dishonor for something we have done or said. It is often described as a conscious awareness or knowing.

Yet from a biblical perspective, shame is much more than just an emotional response or state of thinking. Shame is the primary tool used by the enemy to destroy all creation. For shame ultimately does the opposite of *Ahava* or Agape love. Instead of inviting us into a relationship with God, it isolates us from God, disintegrating our relationship with Him and ultimately with everyone else.

Its power is that we are often blind to the shame we bear because it develops in us before we can even develop the language to name it. Over time we develop defenses that define our negative reactions and behavior to people, situations, or circumstances, yet, never aware that the source of these behaviors is linked to shame.

Dr. Curt Thompson, the author of the "Soul of Shame," writes that,

"One way to approach its essence is to understand it as an undercurrent of sensed emotion...that should we put words to it, we would declare some version of *I am not enough: There is something wrong with me; I am bad, or I don't matter.*"

Whether it began with the first negative word spoken to a toddler, the frustrated sigh of a parent with extremely high expectations of their child, or the absentee parent who was never there. The power of these moments lies not in the description but the emotional imprinting these experiences have on our hearts and mind.

As a result, we often lack the insight that much of our "negative" behavior is tied to this imprinted emotion of shame. Therefore, we label our behavior in the context of something else or someone else, both being external to the shame we carry inside.

A 36-year-old woman with many failed relationships attributes it to a problem with so many cheating men. She agrees that her experiences have made her distrusting of even good men. Although she wants to be married and is praying to God for a good man, she is afraid she will sabotage the relationship because of her "issues" and fear of being hurt and betrayed – which she admits she has already done.

While she may label it under "cheating man," "broken trust," or "a hardened heart," at its core there is a shame narrative of "I am not valuable enough to be loved and protected" which may have existed even before the first act of betrayal.

Yet, shame is more than just a consequence of a sinful state. Shame is the primary means by which sin entered into man's story. It is the invisible and cloaked weapon that already resides in us and blocks our ability to truly love and receive true love.

Before there was sin, there was shame.

I am Eve.

[15]And the Lord God took the man and put him into the Garden of Eden to dress it and to keep it. [16]And the Lord God commanded the man, saying, "Of every tree of the garden thou mayest freely eat:

17But of the tree of the knowledge of good and evil, thou shalt not eat of it: for in the day that thou eatest thereof thou shalt surely die."

18And the Lord God said, "It is not good that the man should be alone; I will make him a helper suitable for him."…22And the rib, which the Lord God had taken from man, made he a woman, and brought her unto the man.23 And Adam said, "This is now bone of my bones, and flesh of my flesh: she shall be called 'Woman,' because she was taken out of Man." 24Therefore shall a man leave his father and his mother, and shall cleave unto his wife: and they shall be one flesh.

25And they were both naked, the man and his wife, and were not ashamed. Genesis 2:15-25

It is interesting that in the beginning, before sin entered in the equation, that God made a point to state that they were unashamed. The Bible does not state that they were naked and happy or naked and free, or even naked and fruitful. No, God purposely placed the word unashamed.

In a world where shame should not exist, why mention it here?

Is it possible that the critical point between love and security and fear and poverty of spirit is the emergence of shame?

We might think that the concept of shame is mentioned here because it reflects how God sees them, but in actuality, it is how Eve and Adam see themselves.

> The serpent's question invites Eve to sort out the answer by herself. Nowhere does the serpent suggest they go to God to check the facts. He is not at all concerned with the truth. He is far more interested in disrupting the relationship between woman, God and the man. The serpent has every intention of exploiting her doubt.
>
> Doubt is planted in a way to discredit not so much Eve's rendition of the facts. It is used to rupture relational connections.
>
> So when we doubt ourselves, especially in the face of what we consider to be important events in our lives, we actually doubt our sense of connection with others, not least with God. We doubt we will be **okay**. To be okay as a human is first and foremost about being connected to God and others. *Excerpt from Soul of Shame by Curt Thompson, MD*

¹Now the serpent was more subtle than any beast of the field which the Lord God had made. And he said unto the woman, "Ye, hath God said, Ye shall not eat of every tree of the garden?"

²And the woman said unto the serpent, "We may eat of the fruit of the trees of the garden: But of the fruit of the tree which is in the midst of the garden, ³God hath said, 'Ye shall not eat of it, neither shall ye touch it, lest ye die.'"

⁴And the serpent said unto the woman, "Ye shall not surely die:

For God doth know that in the day ye eat thereof, then your eyes shall be opened, and ye shall be as gods, knowing good and evil."

Genesis 3:1-4

This is where shame is born. It is not that we believe that God is not an all-powerful and righteous God. Shame causes us to doubt our position or value to God. We question whether we really are as valuable and priceless to Him as he describes in Psalms 119.

This is where sin can enter in. In an effort to minimize the pain that shame brings, we withdraw from God and from relationships. We withdraw our trust, generosity,

> In stating flatly that the woman will not die, the serpent offers her a new rendition of the truth.
>
> To be told that you will be like God may seem like a good thing. I would love to hear that. But the subtle idea is that, given the fruit is forbidden, God does not want you to be like him. God does not want you to have what he has. He does not want you to be as close and as connected to Him as you might think He does. And by further implication, therefore, you are not as important as you think. You, as it turns out, are less than you think. **You. Are. Not. Enough.**

vulnerability, and resources because the risk of confronting that "I really am not enough" is too unbearable a pain to manage.

So, like Eve, we look to other sources for our comfort and security-other sources that seem to satisfy the void and the pain of our shame. Yet, these sources can never provide the unconditional love and security for which we are created. These sources only leave us with a larger void for more shame to fill.

> ⁶*And when the woman saw that the tree was good for food, and that it was pleasant to the eyes, and a tree to be desired to make one wise, she took of the fruit thereof, and did eat, and gave also unto her husband with her; and he did eat.*
>
> ⁷*And the eyes of them both were opened, and they knew that they were naked; and they sewed fig leaves together and made themselves aprons. ⁸And they heard the voice of the Lord God walking in the garden in the cool of the day: and Adam and his wife hid themselves from the presence of the Lord God amongst the trees of the garden.*
>
> ⁹*Then the Lord God called to the man, "Where are you?"*
>
> ¹⁰*He replied, "I heard you walking in the garden, so I hid. I was afraid because I was naked."*
>
> ¹¹*"Who told you that you were naked?" the Lord God asked. "Have you eaten from the tree whose fruit I commanded you not to eat?"*
>
> ¹²*The man replied, "It was the woman you gave me who gave me the fruit, and I ate it."*
>
> *Genesis 3:6-12*

Furthermore, shamed people shame people. Broken hearts break hearts. So, thousands upon thousands of years later, we continue to struggle with the consequence of our efforts to cover our shame and minimize its pain. All the while, we deepen our void, isolate ourselves, and pass shame to others like an infectious virus

If you peel back the layers of your heart and the "issues" that you struggle with, can you identify a shame narrative underneath?

Bookmark: My Shame Narrative

Even as a young girl, I struggled with trust and not because a parent or friend betrayed me or intentionally tried to hurt. Yet, I did not trust anyone to get too close to me or know too much about me, out of fear that I was vulnerable to injury.

I remember writing down my promise to myself that I would make sure that I took care of myself. When no one else could or would, *Ericka* would be there for *Ericka*.

This provided me what I believed to be secure boundaries that kept me safe and allowed me to take care of myself. However, even as a young person, I knew I was missing authenticity in relationships and a free expression of love. My journal entries were pinned with fears of ending my days alone and lonely because no one could stay.

As I aged and marriages and relationships bore the burden of my need to control, I prayed for God to reveal why I was so fearful.

Over time and in a season of brokenness, He revealed that it was not because a parent left or abused me or because a man betrayed me or beat me. It was because of the injuries I experienced due to the choices of others who did not consider me in the fall out. Therefore, it was not the pain of an intentional attack that I feared as much as the damage inflicted by someone's unwise decision which negatively impacted my life although it was never their intention to hurt me.

Whether it was witnessing the chaos and disruption of my parents' divorce or the pathologic grief of my mother for the loss of her father, I had to peel back the layers of my protective walls and identify that my shame narrative was,

I am not important enough to be considered or thought of in the choices made by those close to me.

It was this unspoken and unrecognized imprint on my soul that molded my approach to life, relationships with others, and myself. It kept me from experiencing the freedom of love with all of its joys and all of its risks.

By identifying it, I could give it to God and ask Him to peel away my layers and allow me to forgive those I could not trust, forgive myself for not trusting, and begin to love without fear. Realizing that when all else and all others fail me, He will never fail me.

Let your conduct *be* without covetousness; *be* content with such things as you have. For He Himself has said, "I will never leave you nor forsake you." So, we may boldly say: "The Lord *is* my helper; I will not fear. What can man do to me?" (Hebrews 11:5-6).

Personal Reflection

The Journey toward a Pure Heart.

To confront this shame requires that we risk feeling it on the way to healing. This is not easy and often is the reason for our broken relationships. We do everything we can to protect the pain of dealing with this shame narrative. Yet with any unchartered journey, one cannot start without the first step.

He became shame for us.

God placed himself at the mercy of creation and allowed himself to be bullied, betrayed, beaten, abused, neglected, accused, distressed, and ashamed. He paid the price of shame and sin for us.

Looking unto Jesus, the author and finisher of our faith, who for the joy that was set before Him endured the cross, despising the shame, and has sat down at the right hand of the throne of God. Hebrews 12:2

For He made Him who knew no sin to be sin for us, that we might become the righteousness of God in Him. 2 Corinthians 5:21

He loved us first.

He loves us no matter what. His love never fails. It never turns back. It never abandons us.

In this is love, not that we have loved God but that he loved us and sent his Son to be the propitiation for our sins. 1 John 4:10

[37]No, in all these things we are more than conquerors through him who loved us. [38]For I am sure that neither death nor life, nor angels nor rulers, nor things present nor things to come, nor powers, [39]nor height nor depth, nor anything else in all creation, will be able to separate us from the love of God in Christ Jesus our Lord.

Romans 8:37–39

Love never gives up, never loses faith, is always hopeful, and endures through every circumstance. 1 Corinthians 13:7

He wants to heal us of our shame and give us a new heart so **that we can truly love without fear.**

And I will give you a new heart, and I will put a new spirit in you. I will take out your stony, stubborn heart and give you a tender, responsive heart. Ezekiel 36:26

The Lord is close to the brokenhearted; He rescues those whose spirits are crushed. Psalms 34:18

For God has not given us a spirit of fear, but of power and of love and of a sound mind. 2 Timothy 1:7

We must invite God to search our hearts because we are unaware of the closed-off wounds that have yet to be treated.

⁹The heart is deceitful above all things, and desperately wicked: who can know it? ¹⁰I the Lord search the heart, I try the reins, even to give every man according to his ways, and according to the fruit of his doings. Jeremiah 17:9-10

²³Search me, O God, and know my heart; Try me, and know my anxieties; ²⁴And see if there is any wicked way in me, and lead me in the way everlasting. Psalms 139:23-24

Test me, LORD, and try me, examine my heart and my mind. Psalms 26:2

We must give Him our heart, our mind, and our soul.

The love God requires begins with trusting Him with your heart – all of it. Even when others hurt you, you are afraid or just do not understand, God wants to you to trust that He is for you.

Trust in the LORD with all your heart and lean not on your own under-

standing. Proverbs 3:5

My son, give me your heart and let your eyes delight in my ways. Proverbs 23:26

And the peace of God, which transcends all understanding, will guard your hearts and your minds in Christ Jesus. Philippians 4:7

My flesh and my heart may fail, but God is the strength of my heart and my portion forever. Psalms 73:26

He wants you to know that He loves and values you. He will never leave you undone.

When you truly believe that God is who He says He is and that you are who He says you are, you will then realize it doesn't matter what others do or say…God is enough.

[13]"For I am the Lord, your God, who takes hold of your right hand and says to you, Do not fear; I will help you. [14]Do not be afraid, for I myself will help you," declares the Lord, your Redeemer, the Holy One of Israel. Isaiah 41:13-14

[6]The Lord is with me; I will not be afraid. What can man do to me? [7]The Lord is with me; he is my helper. Psalm 118:6-7

Fear of man will prove to be a snare, but whoever trusts in the Lord is kept safe. Proverbs 29:25

This is when we can love like He loves…because we finally believe that we are loved completely and unconditionally by Him.

No shame.

There is no fear in love. But perfect love drives out fear, because fear has to do with punishment.

1 John 4:8

Chapter 10
What else can you do?

Beth Moore

"Man, oh man, just gonna say there ain't no such thing as invulnerable love. Not on this earth anyway. Not in this skin. To be open to its joys is to be open to its aches and often simultaneously. Therein's the rub but also the beauty. Love is costly but lovelessness is bankruptcy."
Twitter, March 21, 2018

The Great Commandment

> [37] *Jesus replied, "You must love the Lord your God with all your heart, all your soul, and all your mind.'* [38] *This is the first and greatest commandment.* [39] *A second is equally important: 'Love your neighbor as yourself.'* [40] *The entire law and all the demands of the prophets are based on these two commandments."*
>
> *Matthew 22:37-40*

Bookmark: Falling short

When I used to read the great commandment to love the Lord God with all my mind, heart, and strength, I admittedly pictured God as distant from the command. The command makes sense and I agree with God, for He is God and I am His creation. Of course, I should love Him with all of my being.

Yet, such a command, this great command, appeared lofty to me, and honestly, I wasn't sure what that looked like in my actual day to day living. So, I saw it as a goal that I likely wouldn't completely realize until I was in His presence.

Of course, I was a pretty good Christian. I prayed, I read the Bible, I tithed, I was active in church. For the most part, I got along with everyone or eventually repented, if I didn't. Yet something about the Great Commandment left me feeling so far below what I considered to be God's expectation.

So, I just accepted that this must a goal to reach at the end of a long-life, when I am gray-haired, wise, and able to focus on the Lord.
-*Ericka*

The truth is God does not require us to love Him with all of our being for His own enjoyment and satisfaction. It is not because God is so self-absorbed that He must bask in our unending love in order to be satisfied or pleased.

This may sound irreverent, but for many us, this is our silent perception of God, a perception that does not come from a true experience with God. We may harbor this perception of God from experiences in our own relationships which were one-sided and required more from us than what we received in return. Relationships that possibly left us with the question of whether we were enough.

The truth is unless we understand the vital, all-encompassing, and critical magnitude of a loving God, we can never fully receive the liberty in life that God has promised. Until we "see" the power of His love, we will never see the power to declare heaven on earth, move those mountains in our lives, or bring that which has died back to life. We will never understand that all that we hope to be, all that we dream, and all that we envision for those we love, will never be fully realized without this kind of love.

It is more than a smile and a hug. It is more than just a prayer. It is even more than just a sacrifice. It is God in all of His fullness.

By it, all things were created, and all things are sustained, and all things are made new! It is love that brought us back to God. It is love that will bring us home to Him.

He who does not love does not know God, for God is love. 1 John 4:8

> *15He is the image of the invisible God, the firstborn over all creation. 16For by Him all things were created that are in heaven and that are on earth, visible and invisible, whether thrones or dominions or principalities or powers. All things were created through Him and for Him. 17And He is before all things, and in Him all things consist.*
>
> *1 Colossians 1:15-17*

All things were made through Him, and without Him nothing was made that was made. John 1:3

The distance you reach, the heights you attain, the breadth you cover, or the impact of your life is totally dependent on your willingness to receive His love and reflect His love to others.

Love is the language of God and the currency of His kingdom!

The Currency of the Kingdom

From the beginning, man was created for relationship with God. All of creation, the earth, stars, galaxies…all of the universe, was made for us to explore and share with God, for we are the pure object of His love.

In all creation, including the angels and hosts of heaven, only man is made in the image of God. Only man was given dominion and authority over the earth and only man was given the power to choose or reject God.

Even when man rejected God, God's love never stopped. God placed Himself at the mercy of His rejecters, took on our shame and lowered Himself at the feet of man in order to save man.

Yes! You are the object of His pure love and absolutely nothing can separate you from it!

> *[37]Yet in all these things we are more than conquerors through Him who loved us. [38]For I am persuaded that neither death nor life, nor angels nor principalities nor powers, nor things present nor things to come, [39]nor height nor depth, nor any other created thing, shall be able to separate us from the love of God which is in Christ Jesus our Lord.*
>
> *Romans 8:37-39*

So, if God is love and we are commanded to love God with all of our created being, it is not that God is just desirous of sacrificial admiration.

He commanded us to love Him with all of our heart, mind, and strength, so that we could have relationship with Him, for it is the language that He speaks.

The Language of Love

Have you ever visited a country or a people where your language was not spoken? If you have, then you understand the feeling of isolation and awkwardness that you experienced. You found yourself trying to listen for words or expressions that you recognized so that you could join in the conversation.

When you came across someone who spoke your language, you attached yourself to them, so they could provide a sense of home for you. You felt more secure with that person who could explain things, translate for you, or just provide a needed conversation. If you have experienced such a trip, then that person may have even become the fastest best friend you ever made…at least for the duration of the trip.

Being able to talk to someone in a shared language has immediate benefits. It opens up trust. It allows for a greater exchange of accurate information and sharing. It promotes collaboration and teamwork. It builds a relationship.

So, it is with God's love; it is His language; it is His culture, so to speak.

When we are commanded to love Him, it is like He is telling us to learn His language, so that we can trust Him, understand His ways, or just to have a needed conversation.

For it is not for Him to understand us, but for us to understand and know Him.

For to know Him is to love Him and to love Him is to serve Him... and others.

However, because mankind forfeited his relationship with God in the Garden of Eden, the consequences of shame and sin made it impossible for man to truly know God and serve Him.

God's language was so foreign that mankind needed others to translate it and explain God's will. Mankind needed others to lead and direct. Mankind needed others to sacrifice on his behalf; yet never knowing who God was nor understanding His love for them.

Man served out of obligation not true relationship and could not receive the blessings that such a relationship would bring.

And so the Lord says, "These people say they are mine. They honor me with their lips, but their hearts are far from me, and their worship of me is nothing but man-made rules learned by rote." Isaiah 29:13

> *²¹Listen, you foolish and senseless people, with eyes that do not see and ears that do not hear... ²⁴They do not say from the heart, "Let us live in awe of the Lord our God for he gives us rain each spring and fall, assuring us of a harvest when the time is right."*
>
> *²⁵Your wickedness has deprived you of these wonderful blessings. Your sin has robbed you of all these good things.*
>
> *Jeremiah 5:21, 24-25*

Under the old covenant, the priest stands and ministers before the altar day after day, offering the same sacrifices again and again, which can never take away sins. Hebrews 10:11

So, when no earthly mediator could translate God's love to man, He wrapped Himself in flesh and removed the barrier of sin and shame. He placed Himself in our hearts so that we could understand His ways, know His heart, and trust Him with all of ourselves.

33I will put My law in their minds and write it on their hearts; and I will be their God, and they shall be My people. 34No more shall every man teach his neighbor, and every man his brother, saying, "Know the Lord," for they all shall know Me, from the least of them to the greatest of them, says the Lord.

Jeremiah 31:33-34

20By his death, Jesus opened a new and life-giving way through the curtain into the Most Holy Place. 21And since we have a great High Priest who rules over God's house, 22let us go right into the presence of God with sincere hearts, fully trusting him. For our guilty consciences have been sprinkled with Christ's blood to make us clean, and our bodies have been washed with pure water.

Hebrews 10:20-22

When humankind could not make sense of God's laws and commands, Jesus translated the law of God, the heart of God, and made a living and breathing source of love for every believer.

Think not that I am come to destroy the law, or the prophets: I am not come to destroy but to fulfill. Matthew 5:22

When we struggle with anger and bitterness, Jesus translates God's language by revealing even our anger can result in consequences equal to a murderous act.

21Ye have heard that it was said by them of old time. Thou shalt not kill; and whatsoever shall kill shall be in danger of judgment. 22aBut I say to you, that whosoever is angry with his brother without a cause shall in be in danger of the judgment. Matthew 6:21-22a

When we love only those who love us and dislike those who do not,

Jesus translates God's language and tells us to love our enemies and friends as ourselves and bless those who abuse and use us.

43Ye have head that it hath been said, thou shalt love thy neighbor, and hate thine enemy. 44But I say unto you, love your enemies, bless them that curse you, do good to them that hate you, and pray for them which despitefully use you, and persecute you. Matthew 6:43-44

When humankind could only talk to God through the filter of another limited, faulty human, Jesus translated the desires of our hearts to God so that they could be heard.

Wherefore he is able also to save them to the uttermost that come unto God by him, seeing he ever liveth to make intercession for them. Hebrews 7:25

For when we speak God's language, we become more than visiting travelers who continually struggle to find our way. We become family and like family, we can sit at the table of God and receive all that we need from Him – now able to ask Him directly for ourselves.

Jesus replied, "All who love me will do what I say. My Father will love them, and we will come and make our home with each of them." John 14:23

What language are you speaking? How is your love expressed?

Like any language, God's love cannot be learned without an instructor. An instructor who provides the rules of expression and the tone, intent, and action that accompanies it. That instructor is Jesus Christ and through His sacrifice, we can access the heart of God. We can know Him and His love, sacrificing ourselves first unto Him so that He can teach us to love /Ahava/ like He loves us.

1Everyone who believes that Jesus is the Christ has become a child of God. And everyone who loves the Father loves his children, too. 2We know we love God's children if we love God and obey his commandments. 3Loving God means keeping his commandments, and his commandments are not burdensome.

Any other expression is foreign, leading us to seek counterfeit expressions rendering us isolated and defeated.

For every child of God defeats this evil world, and we achieve this victory through our faith. And who can win this battle against the world? Only those who believe that Jesus is the Son of God. John 1:5

"Love, even unto Death, and Live"

Before there were kings, the nation of Israel had Judges ruling over them. It was during this time that Ruth lived. She lived three hundred years before King David came on the scene, yet her life was critical to his life and destiny.

Ruth was not an Israelite. In fact, she was from the nation of Moab that was considered an enemy of Israel and wicked by God. However, her background did not disqualify her from God's plan or purpose for her life.

She and her sister, Orpah, married two men of Israel from the tribe of Judah. The men and their parents, Elimelech and Naomi, had to move to Moab due to a severe famine in Israel.

Yet the story of Ruth's life begins with tragedy and loss. Soon after marriage, she loses her father-in-law, brother-in-law, and her husband. Moreover, her mother-in-law, Naomi, now desires to leave to return to Israel to mourn and die.

As a young widow in those days, she was left with nothing. Without a husband, she had no choices. Unless she returned home with the opportunity to remarry, she would become a beggar, slave, or harlot.

Yet, Ruth decided to stay with Naomi!

Naomi was old, a widow herself, and in a worse state than Ruth. Naomi had no more opportunity to have children and to remarry.

¹²Turn again, my daughters, go your way; for I am too old to have a husband. If I should say, I have hope, if I should have a husband also tonight, and should also bear sons;

¹³Would ye tarry for them till they were grown? would ye stay for them from having husbands? nay, my daughters; for it grieveth me much for your sakes that the hand of the Lord is gone out against me.

¹⁴And they lifted up their voice and wept again: and Orpah kissed her mother in law; but Ruth clave unto her.

Ruth 1:12-14

In spite of all she would lose, and in spite of a future life of poverty and possible death, Ruth went with Naomi back to a land she did not know. In fact, the Bible states that Ruth *cleaved unto* Naomi.

Cleave means "to adhere firmly and closely or loyally and unwaveringly."

The first time the word "cleave" is used in the Bible is in Genesis with the description of the first marriage in history.

Therefore, shall a man leave his father and his mother, and shall cleave *unto his wife: and they shall be one flesh. Genesis 2:24*

So, the same word used to represent the union between a man and a woman in marriage is the same word describing Ruth's commitment to Naomi. In fact, one of the most quoted scriptures in wedding ceremonies is the one spoken by Ruth to Naomi. Not that Ruth was anything more than a widowed daughter in law, but that she sacrificed everything for someone who could never repay. She united her life with Naomi's, for two are better than one.

Although the Bible does not speak about the relationship of Naomi or Ruth before these events, one can believe that Naomi showed Ruth a love that Ruth could not live without. Ruth was willing to put her life at risk for Naomi and all that Naomi represented- her life, her land, and her God.

¹⁶And Ruth said, "Intreat me not to leave thee, or to return from following after thee: for whither thou goest, I will go; and where thou lodgest, I will lodge: thy people shall be my people, and thy God my God.

¹⁷Where thou diest, will I die, and there will I be buried. The Lord do so to me, and more also, if ought but death part thee and me." ¹⁸When she saw that she was steadfastly minded to go with her, then she left speaking unto her.

Ruth 1:16-18

That is what God's love does. It pours into us and changes our hearts so much that we cannot help but pour it back out. As it is poured out, it spreads and reaches. It grows and becomes stronger the more it is expressed and released.

It enlarges one's territory to receive more from God, only to be poured out again as an overflow of love to others.

Love can only grow. Love must multiply!

Have you ever sacrificed much or everything for someone who could not return the sacrifice?

Can you identify a time when such sacrifice, brought a return blessing to your life?

Ruth returned to Bethlehem and worked the fields to gather grain left on the ground by workers of someone else's field. She could have been raped, enslaved, or killed by anyone in the fields but she chose to do it for her and Naomi.

She came across a field that belonged to a man named Boaz. Boaz was related to Naomi's husband and happened to check on the progress of his workers. He noticed Ruth and asked about her. He was told what she had done for Naomi and how hard she worked in the fields.

> *¹⁰Then she fell on her face, and bowed herself to the ground, and said unto him, "Why have I found grace in thine eyes, that thou shouldest take knowledge of me, seeing I am a stranger?"*
>
> *¹¹And Boaz answered and said unto her, "It hath fully been shewed me, all that thou hast done unto thy mother in law since the death of thine husband: and how thou hast left thy father and thy mother, and the land of thy nativity, and art come unto a people which thou knewest not heretofore.*
>
> *¹²The Lord recompense thy work, and a full reward be given thee of the Lord God of Israel, under whose wings thou art come to trust."*
>
> *Ruth 2:10-12*

He had compassion on her. He allowed her to continue collecting grain from his field. He told her to eat and drink what she wanted. He even told his workers to drop extra grain on the ground and allow her to pull grain directly from the plants.

He blessed her because she had blessed someone else. He provided for her because she provided for someone else. He sacrificed his own valued property because she valued someone else.

Naomi realizing Boaz was a relative, instructed Ruth on how to carry herself with Boaz. Boaz followed the tradition of the time and *negotiated* to redeem all of Naomi's husband's and son's property which included taking Ruth as his wife to maintain the legacy of her husband's name.

> *⁹And Boaz said unto the elders, and unto all the people, "Ye are witnesses this day, that I have bought all that was Elimelech's, and all that was Chilion's and Mahlon's, of the hand of Naomi.*
>
> *¹⁰Moreover Ruth the Moabitess, the wife of Mahlon, have I purchased to be my wife, to raise up the name of the dead*

upon his inheritance, that the name of the dead be not cut off from among his brethren, and from the gate of his place: ye are witnesses this day.

Ruth 4:9-10

Ruth was not looking for a husband. She was only trying to survive for herself and Naomi. Without any hope of return, she sacrificed all she knew for someone else, someone who could never repay her gift. She loved unconditionally and generously.

Ruth showed *Âhava*. She "gave" without expecting anything in return. She gave of herself and her life for someone who could not give life back. She gave away her own opportunities, even at the risk of closing the door on her future and wellbeing!

Yet, by opening up her heart and loving someone at the risk of a great loss, her love actually expanded space and opportunity for life. It brought opportunities to her that she could never have imagined. It enlarged her territory and invited more love in, enough love to fill a void not only in her life, but in the life of Naomi.

> [13]*So Boaz took Ruth, and she was his wife: and when he went in unto her, the Lord gave her conception, and she bare a son. And Naomi took the child, and laid it in her bosom, and became nurse unto it.* [14]*And the women, her neighbors gave it a name, saying, "There is a son born to Naomi; and they called his name Obed: he is the father of Jesse, the father of David."*

Ruth 4:13-14

Ruth in Hebrew means "compassionate friend," and she embodied her name in all respects.

Ruth's story shows us that when we give (*Âhava*) of ourselves without thought of what we may lose, we will receive much more than we could ever have imagined.

Ruth left her country empty, without husband, child, or support. She left all she had for one poor widow. Her expression of love brought life, not only in the renewal of Naomi, but in the life of a son who was to be in the bloodline of King David and our savior and eternal King, Jesus Christ.

The impact of her actions changed her life and the lives of those around her. Yet, more astounding is how it changed the course of history "beyond a thousand generations."

If you could see your love perform the miracles in your life and others, like watching water turn to crystalline ice, would you choose to love differently? Would you choose to give God all of your Heart?

If you could see....
If you could see love like water would it change what you would drink?
If love filled every crevice and pit, would you fill every tub and sink?
If you could see love revive all that has died, would you pour it on every dead spot?
If life budded and bloomed from the dirt and dung, would you not let love flow, ... would you not?
If you could bathe in love like water-warm, foamy, and blue, washing away the stink and stain, making all things fresh and new.
Would you let it flow like a river or fall drop by drop?
Would you only wash your feet or be drenched from the bottom to the top?
If you could see love like a great fountain, able to quench the thirst of dying men,
Would you open the well without charge or exchange, and cover a multitude of sins?

-egreene

Chapter 11
A heart condition revisited

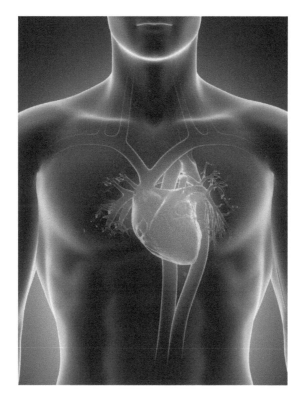

Cardiomyopathy is a disease of heart muscle caused by high blood pressure, blocked arteries, toxins, or infections that damage its muscle.

Although there are different types of cardiomyopathy, the symptoms are similar.

The heart is unable to fill itself with enough blood, and/or the heart is unable to pump enough blood to the rest of the body.

The consequences of cardiomyopathy are very serious and deadly. The lack of oxygenated and sufficient blood flow to the body and its organs causes general deterioration and death.

It is no different than with our spiritual heart.

Often, we are walking around with hearts that are hardened by pressures, sinful toxins, and thus, are not functioning well. A hardened heart is unable to expand to receive life-sustaining blood for itself and unable to pump to nourish the rest of the body.

In the natural, a patient with cardiomyopathy has symptoms related to poor blood flow to the:

-    *Brain*, resulting in strokes, poor vision, deficits in memory and knowledge, poor judgment and emotional decline;

-    *Muscles*, resulting in a lack of endurance, fatigue, weakness; and

-    *Digestive system*, resulting in the inability to process food, to receive nutrition, and to pass toxic waste.

In the spiritual, a person with a hardened heart has symptoms related to limited flow of love to the:

-    *Mind*, resulting in blindness to the things of God and the needs of others. Lack of knowledge and wisdom, accompanied with anxiety and fear;

-    *Heart and strength*, resulting in an inability to withstand spiritual attack, no faith in God, hopelessness and despair; and

-    *Soul*, resulting in an inability to digest and fully comprehend the meat of God's   word, becoming weaker and weaker from not having the bread of life.

A person with a small heart is unable to do much in life. Social interactions and employment are difficult. Helping others is not possible for they themselves require the help of others. Their lives become small and limited to the demands of their sick heart – doctor appointments, procedures, medicines, caretakers, etc.

A person with a spiritually small heart remains blind to their limited capacity but also blind to what God is doing in their life and the lives of others. They miss God and the opportunities around them. They are unable to hear His voice and recognize His will. Worse, they cannot hear or see anyone else beyond their own condition because they can only focus on their own issues.

26Go and say to this people:

When you hear what I say,

you will not understand.

When you see what I do,

you will not comprehend.

27For the hearts of these people are hardened,

and their ears cannot hear,

and they have closed their eyes—

so their eyes cannot see,

and their ears cannot hear,

and their hearts cannot understand,

and they cannot turn to me

and let me heal them.

Acts 28:26-27.

17Live no longer as the Gentiles do, for they are hopelessly confused. 18Their minds are full of darkness; they wander far from the life God gives because they have closed their minds and hardened their hearts against him. 19They have no sense of shame. They live for lustful pleasure and eagerly practice every kind of impurity.

Ephesian 4:17-19

With God, we have the ability to pour God's love into people and change lives. Even if we never say a word, preach a sermon, pray a prayer – just one gesture of unmerited love shown toward one person can heal one person, one family, and even a nation.

If you could see what God has for you

Give, and it will be given to you: good measure, pressed down, shaken together, and running over will be put into your bosom. For with the same measure that you use, it will be measured back to you. Luke 6:38

Have you ever struggled with loving someone or sacrificing for someone unconditionally? Why?

Often our ability to love without condition, is limited by the fear of what we may lose in the process:

- Fear of being rejected;

- Fear of having less;

- Fear of looking bad;

- Fear, fear, fear, etc.

Yet, the love that comes from God can never contain fear because fear will always be about self.

The nature of fear, no matter the context, will always trigger the need to protect ourselves. Choose any situation where fear is present, and it will be associated with a desire to protect yourself from loss or injury.

In fact, the opposite of "love" is not "hate." The opposite of love is self-ishness, and selfishness is rooted in fear.

The reason why we must learn to love as God commands is because love ushers in so many blessings. Love is fertile – it grows and multi-plies. Love is active – it moves and travels. Love is eternal – the impact of love will be seen in eternity.

Fear (and selfishness) ushers in the opposite. Instead of protecting you from what you fear, it actually invites it in your life, in one form or the other.

In Matthew Chapter 25, Jesus talks about a man who gave his three servants bags of gold to invest on his behalf. The two who invested (gave to support something else), gained double in return. However, the third servant who decided to bury his gold because of his fear had his gold taken away.

> [24]*"Master, I knew you were a harsh man, harvesting crops you didn't plant and gathering crops you didn't cultivate.* [25]*I was afraid I would lose your money, so I hid it in the earth. Look, here is your money back." **** [28]*Then he ordered, "Take the money from this servant, and give it to the one with the ten bags of silver.* [29]*To those who use well what they are given, even more will be given, and they will have abundance. But from those who do nothing, even what lit-tle they have will be taken away.* [30]*Now throw this useless servant into outer darkness, where there will be weeping and gnashing of teeth."*
>
> *Matthew 25:24-25, 28-30*

Out of fear of loss, he lost what he had and so much more.

Have you ever been confronted with the one thing that you feared and worked so hard to avoid?

What God wants us to understand and experience is that to love sacrificially does not cause us to lose but to gain. Love only multiplies. It never subtracts.

In fact, God returns not only what you gave, but you receive it multiplied and in ways you never could have imagined or dreamed.

Give, and you will receive. Your gift will return to you in full pressed down, shaken together to make room for more, running over, and poured into your lap. The amount you give will determine the amount you get back. Luke 6:38

God's command for us to love (to give) is not to take from us but to allow Him to pour into our lives and those around us, so much so, that we could never begin to measure the abundance.

No eye has seen, no ear has heard, and no mind has imagined what God has prepared for those who love him. 1 Corinthians 2:9

The returns of love are much too great to lose!

If you could see what God has for others.

Nothing is wasted with God. As He pours into us, we cannot help but pour into those around us. Love never stops moving. It is always growing and spreading.

Love is like water; it will find every space, every crack, and fill it. There is no rock or stone that can withstand it. There is no mountain that is not swallowed by it. No matter the circumstances, love, like water, never changes its substance.

So, if God's love is allowed to pour into us to overflowing, then the run-off is for everyone else.

You become a vessel for God's love to be spread to those around you. God's love in and God's love out—ever-flowing.

The woman at the well was thirsty. She was not just thirsty for a drink but thirsty for real love, security, and respect. She was an outcast because of her promiscuous lifestyle yet she still yearned for something to quench her "thirst." Jesus met her where she was – in shame and despair and offered her a water that would never run dry.

> [10]Jesus replied, "If you only knew the gift God has for you and who you are speaking to, you would ask me, and I would give you living water…[14]But those who drink the water I give will never be thirsty again. It becomes a fresh, bubbling spring within them, giving them eternal life."
>
> John 4:10, 14

A thirsty woman found the love of Jesus and ran to those who discarded her, pleaded with those who disrespected her, and led those who abandoned her, to the source of water that never stops flowing.

If you could see what God has for the world

Lastly, when we learn to love as God commands, God changes our hearts into His heart.

But if we love each other, God lives in us, and his love is brought to full expression in us. 1 John 4:12

[16]We know how much God loves us, and we have put our trust in his love. God is love, and all who live in love, live in God, and God lives in them. [17]And as we live in God, our love grows more perfect. 1 John 4:16-17

This is the only way that we can love others like He does. It is not in our power to love others so unconditionally. Only when we give God all of our heart, can He do what He desires with it.

His desire is to use you to speak life in dead places, renew faith in hopeless situations, and pour love into a hardened heart.

The return for such sacrifice is beyond what can be spoken of or measured. For there are blessings that are untold which are reserved for those who love God and others.

For with such love, we cast out all fear (*1 John 4:18*).

With such love, we can cover a multitude of sins (*1 Peter 4:8*).

With such love, we will see Him (*Matthew 5:8*).

With such love, we will know Him (*Colossians 3:10; 1 Corinthians 2:16*).

With such love, we open the door for God to bless beyond your life, for a thousand generations.

But I lavish unfailing love for a thousand generations on those who love me and obey my commands. Exodus 20:6

Bookmark: "How Good Can It Be?"

In 2010, Oprah Winfrey discovered that she had a half-sister. Nine years after Oprah was born, Oprah's mother gave birth to a baby girl she immediately put up for adoption in 1963. Patricia bounced around from one foster home to another before being adopted. She spent decades wondering about her birth mother and biological family. Then, in 2007, Patricia requested her birth records and learned that she had three biological siblings.

One day, Patricia saw a local news story interviewing Oprah's mother, Vernita Lee. Patricia noticed that many of the details Vernita shared lined up exactly with what she had read in her birth records. Her efforts to reach her mother initially failed. When she finally made contact, her mother refused to meet her. She finally contacted a cousin and DNA tests confirmed the relation: Patricia had found her biological family. Vernita Lee was her mother and Oprah Winfrey, her older sister.

Patricia's journey was more than just about the gift of finding her birth family, it was about being able to love without resentment and anger during that journey. This allowed her to not only survive but thrive so she could pour that same love into her own children and other foster children like herself.

Her loving heart also brought a blessing to Oprah. Patricia never sold her story, tried to blackmail Oprah, seek wealth or position from her famous sister. Patricia was able to give unconditional love to Oprah, who had already experienced betrayal at the hands of those she called family. Patricia just wanted a relationship. She just wanted a sister's love.

She received that, and so much more.

In the end, the blessings were so abundant that all Patricia could say is.

How good can it be?"

https://www.youtube.com/watch?v=TbPofBe5Ffw (*'How good can it be?"*

https://www.youtube.com/watch?v=dwul-Cxr1js&t=46s   *(Oprah's gift to Patricia)*

https://www.huffingtonpost.com/2013/07/25/oprahs-sister-patricia-lee_n_3647985.html

Personal Reflection

Love is giving what you do not have.

This is the mystery that God wants to reveal.

When you give away what you do not have or have very little of, such sacrifice, opens up your heart so that He can fill that void.

We hold on to our hurts so tightly, that we cannot forgive or love without judgment or pride. Yet, we still secretly want the hurt to be healed.

The mystery is that when you give the love that you have not received or when you sacrifice yourself for others when no one sacrificed for you, you are opening your heart to God.

You demonstrate your love for God, by choosing to think like Him (all your mind), feel like HIM (all of your heart), and act like Him (all of your strength).

This allows God to pour into your heart and change it —removing the stones of hurt, pride, and anger and replacing them with peace, gratitude, and joy.

In the natural, it brings life to dead relationships, attracting people and things in your life that bless you instead of curse you.

Like the discarded woman in the Bible, for whom no one comforted or cared for, she poured her precious alabaster oil on Jesus's feet, washed them with her tears, and dried them with her hair. She gave to Him all that she had and that which she could not afford to lose. In return, she was healed of her sin and shame. It was her sacrificial love for Jesus that covered a multitude of her sins.

Therefore, I say to you, her sins, which are many, are forgiven, for she loved much. But to whom little is forgiven, the same loves little. Luke 7:48

Through the brokenness of your life and the pain you may have experienced at the hands of those who should have loved you, can you love?

Can you trust God again with your heart, loving Him and His will for your life at the expense of your defenses and fear?

If you can, He has an abundance of love, healing, and joy that He wants to pour into those broken and dark places.

For He made you in love, and He wants to pour that love back into your heart.

He wants you to love those around you even if you do not get it back in return, for His return is more than enough!

Prayer

Lord, Jesus, search my heart and my mind. If You find evil, Lord lead me in your righteous way everlasting

Lord I repent of the sin of anger, unforgiveness, and resentment that I have carried against others. I repent for justifying my selfishness and unwillingness to give an apology or forgive a wrongdoing because of my fear and pride. Lord, I renounce the shame that says that I am a victim and unworthy-that I am not enough. I cast my shame off, and I put on Christ where my identity and purpose dwell.

Lord, I now ask that You abide in my heart. I give You my heart. Dwell in me and take control. Fill me with Your Holy Spirit and saturate me with Your love, that I may think like You, act like You, and love like You.

Expand my territory and stretch my capacity. Make me a worthy vessel to be used in the overflow to my family, to my community, unto a 1000 generations!

In Jesus' name. Amen

Section 4
Where have you been positioned?

"You may not control all the events that happen to you, but you can decide not to be reduced by them." – Maya Angelou

Chapter 12
Pawns and Promises

Historically, women have been subjected to positions of servitude, second-hand status, and submission – often at the hands of those closest to them or entrusted to protect them.

Unfortunately, everyone knows of a female who has been victimized, abused, or neglected in a situation that she never intentionally sought for herself. This is not to discount the stories of all victims, male or female, yet a greater proportion of women and girls are targets for such situations. Possibly, it is because the female is physically weaker and more vulnerable, or maybe it is because women are viewed as objects of beauty or a prize to obtain. Yet, history has shown that for all these reasons and more, women and girls are often the victims of other people's agendas and desires. Often placed in positions that they never wanted, pressed in corners from which they cannot escape, or pinned to walls as showpieces for someone else's glory.

The beautiful, slim wife and mother with a picture-perfect husband and family yet suffering severe abuse and neglect hidden behind her perfect smile; unable to leave her only source of security.

The 18-year-old who can't leave the "only person who loves me" even though his love has left her diseased and infertile and unable to process the loss of unborn life she carried for a moment.

The 14-year-old girl who obsesses about her body and dress for fear her boyfriend will look or go after another girl.

The 23-year-old who shares an apartment with two other young women and their children – all supporting themselves by seeking "clients" at the "hot spots" around town. She wants to be a nurse but never seems to get around to starting the college application that she is always talking about.

Whether a person is positioned in a place of vulnerability due to physical, financial, or even psychological constraints, the common theme is fear and hopelessness.

Fear and hopelessness are toxic states separately but are deadly when combined. Fear, as we discussed in the last chapter, is really the opposite of love. Fear eventually leads to death in a stepwise fashion.

From physical or verbal outbursts to protective defenses, fear takes one on a torturous journey that eventually leads to death – death of relationships, death of reason, death of dreams, death of faith and death of hope. When one has lost hope, then death soon follows.

Hope deferred makes the heart sick, but a dream fulfilled is a tree of life.
Proverbs 13:12

This is the abused child, numb to the pain she has endured, and now unable to respond to any outreach of love.

This is the victim of sex-trafficking who keeps returning to it time after time because normal life seems foreign and she feels unable to return back to the life she once knew.

When we have been placed in positions of restriction or submitted to painful situations that feel inescapable, the first response is fear. Yet if we remain in these places, fear can paralyze us to not move because of more fear. This can lead to hopelessness, and hopelessness turns to death.

Yet, it is easy to understand such a state with examples of an abused woman or a sex traffic victim. If we are honest, our own personal experiences in life have positioned us in places from which we feel that we cannot move, for fear of more pain, loss, or failure. Over time if nothing changes, we can feel helpless to life's circumstances and stuck in our situation. We feel that our efforts are futile and give up having a hope for change, or "escape." We become numb to our lives and that of others.

We become the true *"walking dead"* just going through the motions, not really expecting things to change and hopeless that any effort can make a change.

Can you identify a time when you felt trapped by your circumstances or from fear of failure or pain?

What was your emotional response?

Did you come out of it? For the better or the worse?

What Is Learned Helplessness?

Martin Seligman studied learned helplessness in 1967. His research focused on how learned helplessness was one of the leading causes of depression. Seligman's most famous study of learned helplessness involved dogs that were trained to escape or assume helplessness in response to a negative stimulus.

Seligman's study involved using a device to administer an electric shock to a dog that was kept in a small box shaped cage. The dogs were allowed to jump over a small divider in the box in order to avoid the electric shock. As expected, the dogs would all jump away from the side they could be shocked on in order to avoid this unpleasant experience.

Researchers then administered the shock to dogs that were harnessed to the side of the box the shock was being administered on.

Researchers noted that dogs strapped to the box eventually stopped trying to escape the shock.

Once a dog was shocked enough times without the opportunity to escape, they would stop trying to get away from the shock. This response was strong enough that dogs repeatedly shocked would stop trying to escape even when the straps were removed.

The dogs had effectively learned that resistance was futile, even when it wasn't. Dogs that were later unstrapped and did not try to escape were effectively self-inducing the shock. Once the straps were removed, these dogs could have easily gotten away. They didn't, simply because they didn't try.

http://everythingweknowsofar.com/2016/07/19/want-overcoming-learned-helplessness/

#MeTooinJerusalem

Six to seven hundred years after the time of Jacob and Tamar, there was another Tamar. Her story begins at the age of 19. She was the beautiful virgin daughter of King David. Even before her father became the King of all Israel, he had wives and children. Tamar and her brother Absalom were the 3rd and 4th children of King David by his third wife.

Once David conquered all of his enemies and God gave him the kingdom, King David had many more wives and concubines and more children including Solomon, his seventh son, who would eventually take his Father's place on the throne.

From the biblical account, Tamar did nothing wrong. She deceived no one, did not lie and did not cheat. She did not seek opportunity. She did not consent. Yet unbeknownst to Tamar, there were arrangements and decisions being made for which she had no idea or input, but they would alter her life forever.

This is Tamar's story:

> *¹Now David's son Absalom had a beautiful sister named Tamar. ²And Amnon, her half-brother, fell desperately in love with her. Amnon became so obsessed with Tamar that he became ill. She was a virgin, and Amnon thought he could never have her.*
>
> *³But Amnon had a very crafty friend—his cousin Jonadab. He was the son of David's brother Shimea. ⁴One day Jonadab said to Amnon, "What's the trouble? Why should the son of a king look so dejected morning after morning?" So Amnon told him, "I am in love with Tamar, my brother Absalom's sister."*
>
> *⁵"Well," Jonadab said, "I'll tell you what to do. Go back to bed and pretend you are ill. When your father comes to see you, ask him to let Tamar come and prepare some food for you. Tell him you'll feel better if she prepares it as you watch and feeds you with her own hands."*

6 So Amnon lay down and pretended to be sick. And when the king came to see him, Amnon asked him, "Please let my sister Tamar come and cook my favorite dish as I watch. Then I can eat it from her own hands." 7 So, David agreed and sent Tamar to Amnon's house to prepare some food for him.

8 When Tamar arrived at Amnon's house, she went to the place where he was lying down so he could watch her mix some dough. Then she baked his favorite dish for him. 9 But when she set the serving tray before him, he refused to eat. "Everyone get out of here," Amnon told his servants. So, they all left.

10 Then he said to Tamar, "Now bring the food into my bedroom and feed it to me here." So, Tamar took his favorite dish to him. 11 But as she was feeding him, he grabbed her and demanded, "Come to bed with me, my darling sister."

12 "No, my brother!" she cried. "Don't be foolish! Don't do this to me! Such wicked things aren't done in Israel. 13 Where could I go in my shame? And you would be called one of the greatest fools in Israel. Please, just speak to the king about it, and he will let you marry me."

14 But Amnon wouldn't listen to her, and since he was stronger than she was, he raped her. 15 Then suddenly Amnon's love turned to hate, and he hated her even more than he had loved her. "Get out of here!" he snarled at her.

16 "No, no!" Tamar cried. "Sending me away now is worse than what you've already done to me." But Amnon wouldn't listen to her. 17 He shouted for his servant and demanded, "Throw this woman out, and lock the door behind her!"

18 So the servant put her out and locked the door behind her. She was wearing a long, beautiful robe, as was the custom in those days for the king's virgin daughters. But now Tamar tore her robe and put ashes on her head. And then, with her face in her hands, she went away crying.

2 Samuel 13:1-18

A Pawn in Someone Else's Chess Game

The Pawn

As horrible as Tamar's story is, the backdrop to these events is even more horrible. For until she was raped, her existence was as it had always been. She was the beautiful young daughter of the King. Her royal robes and coverings signified not only her royalty but also her purity. All who saw her would immediately recognize her position and value. Her purity was priceless, and her life was on a path for security, marriage, and lineage in the kingdom.

Yet, she was unaware that the course of her life was about to change. For people who she cared about and trusted were making decisions about her life for which she had no input or control. She was a pawn in someone else's game…the worse kind of betrayal and the worse kind of pain.

She was unaware that there were events which occurred before she was born; events that were lining up to this moment. These events had nothing to do with her, but they directly affected her.

Caught in A Web

David was a man after God's heart. He was brave and full of faith and God anointed him king when he was still a boy in the field. Yet David had issues. He was the youngest son and the least valued. The King gave his daughter, David's wife, to another man. This King, who David considered as a father-figure, accused him of being a traitor and an

Oh, what a **tangled** web we weave… When first we practice to deceive.

– SIR WALTER SCOTT, 1808

outlaw. David was later dismissed by a wealthy crude man and in response, was going to murder his whole household were it not for the man's wife Abigail who soothed his temper. Yes, David had issues, understandably. He struggled with being affirmed and respected despite the favor of God upon his life.

This was manifested in his appetite for women. Before he became King of all of Israel, he had six sons and one daughter by three women (one of them was the widow Abigail). Yet after he was lifted as King, he sought many more wives and concubines, although scriptural law warned against this behavior for kings.

The king must not take many wives for himself, because they will turn his heart away from the Lord. And he must not accumulate large amounts of wealth in silver and gold for himself. Deuteronomy 17:17

It was his appetite that would cause David to fall and cause many to fall with him.

Instead of going to war with his men as kings did, David took a rest and saw Bathsheba bathing. He took her for himself although she was the wife of one of his thirty mighty men who committed their lives to protect David and the kingdom. His name was Uriah.

Uriah was one of thirty men who fought alongside David and defended him with their lives. From the time that David was running for his life from King Saul to the establishment of his kingdom, these great men of valor were so important to his journey, that the Bible lists them by name (*2 Samuel 23:18-39*).

Bathsheba became pregnant and David hid his paternity by having Uriah set up to be killed in battle. David married Bathsheba but God judged David and the child soon died.

Although God spared David, the consequences of his actions would have rippling effects.

This is what the Lord says: "Because of what you have done, I will cause your own household to rebel against you. I will give your wives to another man before your very eyes, and he will go to bed with them in public view. You did it se-

cretly, but I will make this happen to you openly in the sight of all Israel."

2 Samuel 12:11

David's oldest son, Ammon, lusted after his half-sister Tamar, and robbed her of her dignity, virginity, and future. Her father, David, did nothing. Tamar's brother, Absalom, later killed Ammon for his acts. He then sought to take over his father's kingdom under the advice of David's trusted counselor, fulfilling God's prophetic judgment.[4] This same advisor happened to be Bathsheba's grandfather (2 Samuel 23:34; 2 Samuel 11:3).

> [21]*Ahithophel told him, "Go and sleep with your father's concubines, for he has left them here to look after the palace. Then all Israel will know that you have insulted your father beyond hope of reconciliation, and they will throw their support to you."* [22]*So, they set up a tent on the palace roof where everyone could see it, and Absalom went in and had sex with his father's concubines.* [23]*Absalom followed Ahithophel's advice, just as David had done. For every word Ahithophel spoke seemed as wise as though it had come directly from the mouth of God.*

2 Samuel 16:21-23

After these series of events, nothing more is spoken of this Tamar in the Bible. She went to live the rest of her life in her brother's house.

Her brother Absalom saw her and asked, "Is it true that Amnon has been with you? Well, my sister, keep quiet for now, since he's your brother. Don't you worry about it." So Tamar lived as a desolate woman in her brother Absalom's house. 1 Samuel 13:20

She was put in a position that she never wanted or planned. She likely never realized she was ultimately a victim of her father's bruised soul and metastatic sins. Yet, if we stop at this story, we might struggle with the idea that her life was damaged beyond repair and without

---

4   Sleeping with the king's concubines and wives is a way of taking over the kingdom.

hope of recovery or restoration.

How do we reconcile Tamar's story with the promises of God?

Have you experienced a prison-like situation from which you felt you could not escape, whether mental or physical?

Personal Reflection

The truth is that God's plan for our lives is good (*Jeremiah 29:11*) and his promises are **yes** and **amen** (*2 Corinthians 1:20*). No matter the positions that we have been placed, God is bigger than our circumstances. He is stronger than our prisons. He is with us in an open field and He is with us in the hidden, dark, and small spaces.

> *⁷I can never escape from your Spirit! I can never get away from your presence!*
>
> *⁸If I go up to heaven, you are there; if I go down to the grave, you are there.*
>
> *⁹ If I ride the wings of the morning, if I dwell by the farthest oceans,*
>
> *¹⁰even there your hand will guide me, and your strength will support me.*
>
> *¹¹ I could ask the darkness to hide me and the light around me to become night—*
>
> *¹²* **but even in darkness I cannot hide from you.** *To you the night shines as bright as day. Darkness and light are the same to you.*
>
> *Psalms 139:7-12*

He never leaves nor forsakes us (*Joshua 1:5*). Although we may have been pawns in someone else's game or forced in circumstances beyond our initial control, God's will is not bound by these circumstances. His story for you is not over.

God's story for Joseph was not over. Joseph went from the field, to the slave house, to prison, despite the promise over his life that was revealed by his dreams. He was positioned in places beyond his control, yet God used it for His will and plan and when ready, positioned him to his anointed place.

God's story for David was not over. David was the least of his brothers, left to tend the flocks while his brothers were esteemed as warriors and kings. He was ignored and dismissed for just being David. Yet God's calling on his life was fixed. Even though his heart was "positioned" for sin, God still anointed him king and kept his lineage on the throne where Christ would eventually be positioned to reign for eternity.

But from now on the Son of Man will be seated in the place of power at God's right hand. Luke 22:9

The story of a crucified Christ was not over. Before Christ was placed on the throne, He was positioned in a place of torment and torture at the hands of others with their own agendas. Yet, He trusted who He was and the purpose for which He was put in this position. He was resurrected from the grave with all power and glory. He now has the key to set all of us free from the prisons of life.

He was oppressed and treated harshly, yet he never said a word.

He was led like a lamb to the slaughter. And as a sheep is silent before the shearers,

He did not open his mouth. Isaiah 53:7

And Jesus came and spake unto them, saying, All power is given unto Me in heaven and in earth Matthew 28:18

And then I heard every creature in heaven and on earth and under the earth and in the sea. They sang: "Blessing and honor and glory and power belong to the one sitting on the throne and to the Lamb forever and ever." Revelation 5:13

The Spirit of the Lord God is upon me; because the Lord hath anointed me to preach good tidings unto the meek; he hath sent me to bind up the brokenhearted, to proclaim liberty to the captives, and the opening of the prison to them that are bound. Isaiah 61:1

Even in the prisons and places where we have felt helpless and hopeless, God is there. He has a plan. Despite what man has done and despite what we have done, God is faithful and ever-present.

For us to survive and thrive, we must trust and continually place our hope in His faithfulness.

He can lift us out of the deep well.

He can "checkmate" us out of despair.

He can break open our prison doors.

He can fulfill our promise in the midst of

any position we are in.

When he sees all that is accomplished by his anguish, he will be satisfied. And because of his experience, my righteous servant will make it possible for many to be counted righteous, for he will bear all their sins. Isaiah 53:11

The key is to stay faithful and obey the God of your salvation and hope.

[8]Though He was a Son, yet He learned obedience by the things, which He suffered. [9]And having been perfected, He became the author of eternal salvation to all who obey Him, [10]called by God as High Priest according to the order of Melchizedek. Hebrews 5:8-10

Chapter 13
The Promise Hidden in
a Position of Pain

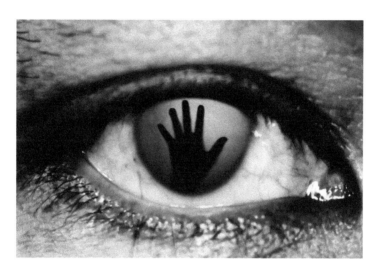

There are situations in life that can feel like a prison. We are stuck and unable to move or we are tied down and can't get free. It does not matter why we are placed in these positions, since what we feel is the same – frustration, helplessness, depression, anxiety, or just numbness.

These prisons can be physical (prison, addiction, disease/disability), mental (regret, anxiety, depression, fear), social (bullying, shame, isolation), and financial (poverty, debt, lack of social mobility). Regardless, prisons of any kind are uncomfortable and undesirable. By their nature, prisons are restrictive and leave little space for stretching or just walking away, free.

Yet, if God has plans for us, plans that are good, then how do we reconcile good plans with hard places and bad positions? How do we answer the following questions or give wise counsel to the following statements?

How long before things change?

What did I do to deserve this?

Who else can take care of them? I am the only one.

My life is made up of pills and doctor appointments. I am so tired.

I can't leave. I have no other place to go.

Mom, I don't feel good, I can't go to school. Please don't make me go.

You don't understand. He's just stressed. He's really very sweet. He really does love me.

I just want to go away. I can't tell anyone. No one will understand. I just want to die.

The answer is that no matter what pressing position you have been placed or situation you have had to endure, the promises of God did not die. His will and plans for you did not change. Such situations may be the darkest chapters of your life, but they are not the whole story and definitely not the conclusion.

The key is to recognize that there is a promise upon your life and God keeps His promise.

For all the promises of God in Him are Yes, and in Him Amen, to the glory of God through us. 2 Corinthians 1:20

El Roi – "The God Who Sees Me"

Abram was called by God to leave his country and family and dwell in a land that he did not own. God promised him that despite his old age, he would be a father of many nations, so much so that it would be impossible to count. Abram believed although he would not live to see it.

[3] Then Abram said, "Look, You have given me no offspring;

indeed one born in my house is my heir!"

⁴And behold, the word of the Lord came to him, saying, "This one shall not be your heir, but one who will come from your own body shall be your heir." ⁵Then He brought him outside and said, "Look now toward heaven, and count the stars if you are able to number them." And He said to him, "So shall your descendants be." ⁶And he believed in the Lord, and He accounted it to him for righteousness.

Genesis 15:3-6

Abram's wife, Sarai, was in her late 70's and past her childbearing years. So, she offered her maidservant Hagar to sleep with Abram so that she could have a child through her (the earliest recorded surrogate mother).

Hagar became pregnant and then despised Sarai. Abram allowed Sarai to punish Hagar severely. So, Hagar ran away to escape but she could go no further than a spring of water in the wilderness. The angel of the Lord appears. He asks her about her tight predicament – a slave girl alone in the wilderness.

⁷Now the Angel of the Lord found her by a spring of water in the wilderness, by the spring on the way to Shur. ⁸And He said, "Hagar, Sarai's maid, where have you come from, and where are you going?" She said, "I am fleeing from the presence of my mistress Sarai."

Genesis 16:7-8

Have you ever had to face a decision to leave or run away from a bad situation that was beyond your control?

Whether you left or not, were there gains and losses?

Even in this situation, God not only had a promise for Abram and Sarai. He had a promise for Hagar.

⁹The Angel of the Lord said to her, "Return to your mistress, and submit yourself under her hand." ¹⁰Then the Angel of the Lord said to her, "I will multiply your descendants exceedingly, so that they shall not be counted for multitude." ¹¹And the Angel of the Lord said to her:

"Behold, you are with child, and you shall bear a son. You shall call his name Ishmael, Because the Lord has heard your affliction. ¹²He shall be a wild man; His hand shall be against every man, And every man's hand against him. And he shall dwell in the presence of all his brethren."

Genesis 16:9-12

Hagar would have a son and her son would not only live but he would thrive.

Yet the promise wasn't without its challenges, for this son would be quarrelsome and have a life full of strife. Today we see this strife manifest in the centuries-old conflict between the nations of Israel (Jacob) and Islam nations (Ishmael) – derived from the two sons of Abraham.

It is important to know that when we sin and choose paths that God has not chosen for us, there are consequences that are inevitable and can affect a thousand generations. Yet, He is full of mercy, providing favor and promise despite our faithless actions. For all things work together for the good to those who love God and called according to his purpose (*Romans 8:28*).

Therefore, the stops, the detours, and the stalls of your life do not have to define your story or its final chapter. There is a promise that lives in the prison-like places of your life. The key is to recognize it and trust God's will for you, for He is listening and sees it all.

¹³Then she called the name of the Lord who spoke to her, You–Are–the God–Who–Sees; for she said, "Have I also here seen Him who sees me?"

¹⁴Therefore the well was called Beer Lahai Roi; observe it is between Kadesh and Bered. Genesis 16:13-14⁵

---

5   El Roi means God sees.

How do we discover the "promise" in our own lives?

How do we recognize God in the midst of such circumstances?

Hindsight is rarely 20/20 and by its definition, it never exists at the beginning. There is often no clarity to the reasons or the purpose of what we experience in life. Often, we are just trying to keep our head above water; trying to survive another day and wondering when it will end.

Likely, Hagar had no idea of the outcome of these events. There was no way she could "see" the impact of this situation on her future, and definitely not the future of the world.

Ishmael was indeed born and was Abraham's only son. Yet, God's promise that Abraham's seed would come from his own body did not include Hagar. His promise was that the seed that would lead to the nation of Israel would come from Abram and Sarai, not Hagar. As God promised, thirteen years later Sarai conceives a son and gives birth to Isaac when she is 90 and Abraham is 100, but there remains a promise for Ishmael.

> *[17] Then Abraham fell on his face and laughed, and said in his heart, "Shall a child be born to a man who is one hundred years old? And shall Sarah, who is ninety years old, bear a child?" [18] And Abraham said to God, "Oh, that Ishmael might live before You!" [19] Then God said: "No, Sarah your wife shall bear you a son, and you shall call his name Isaac; I will establish My covenant with him for an everlasting covenant, and with his descendants after him. [20] And as for Ishmael, I have heard you. Behold, I have blessed him, and will make him fruitful, and will multiply him exceedingly. He shall beget twelve princes, and I will make him a great nation."*
>
> *Genesis 17:17-20*

Once Isaac was born, things worsened for Hagar and her son. Ishmael mocked Isaac, likely jealous of his half-brother who would receive his father's inheritance and blessing. Sarah demanded that Hagar and Ishmael be thrown out. Although this grieved Abraham, God reminded him of his promise for Isaac and Ishmael and told him to send them away.

Whatever Sarah has said to you, listen to her voice; for in Isaac your seed shall be called. Yet I will also make a nation of the son of the bondwoman, because he is your seed. Genesis 21:13

With only bread and water, the food of prison, Hagar and Ishmael were thrown out to the wild. Once her food and water were gone, Hagar gave up and she threw Ishmael (cast him) under a shrub and left him. She walked a far distance, so she could not see him die.

[15]And the water in the skin was used up, and she placed the boy under one of the shrubs. [16a]Then she went and sat down across from him at a distance of about a bowshot; for she said to herself, "Let me not see the death of the boy." Genesis 21:15-16a

Where is the promise in this situation? Where is the favor of God?

How does God's will manifest when we are positioned in death-like situations?

Hagar was blinded by grief and fear, no longer able to see hope in the eyes of her son or obtain comfort from her master's home. Yet her promise remained.

> *[16b]So, she sat opposite him, and lifted her voice and wept.*
>
> *[17]And God heard the voice of the lad. Then the angel of God called to Hagar out of heaven, and said to her, "What ails you, Hagar? Fear not, for God has heard the voice of the lad where he is. [18]Arise, lift up the lad and hold him with your hand, for I will make him a great nation."*
>
> *[19]Then God opened her eyes, and she saw a well of water. And she went and filled the skin with water and gave the lad a drink. [20]So, God was with the lad; and he grew and*

*dwelt in the wilderness and became an archer. ^{21}He dwelt
in the Wilderness of Paran; and his mother took a wife for
him from the land of Egypt.*

Genesis 21:16b-21

Hagar's promise was in her son. She could not see it in the midst of her
dire situation. She forgot or did not understand what the angel of the
Lord told her. Yet the promise of God, the purpose of God, remained
hidden in a bastard son who was never supposed to be born.

Interestingly, it wasn't Hagar's cries to which God responded. He heard
and responded to the cries of the child. The "promise" declared itself.
The promise called to its promise keeper and God listened. ("Ishmael"
means God listens.)

Your promise remains. Even when you are blind to what God is doing
and what blessings He has placed in your life, your promise will declare itself. If you listen and obey, you will see it and be blessed. If you
do not obey, you may forfeit seeing the blessing of the promise. Yet,
the promise remains.

> The Hebrews did not enter the Promise Land due to disobedi-
> ence. God kept his promise to their children (*Hebrews 3:16-19*).

> Rebekah schemed to ensure Jacob was given the inheritance and
> blessing over her other son and ended up losing both them. Yet
> God's promise over her sons remained (*Genesis 27:42-45*).

You see whether Hagar lifted the boy up or not, he would have survived. She may not have, but he would, because God promised.

Hagar in fact did listen to God. When she lifted her son's hand, her
eyes were opened to discover a well of water and they both were re-
plenished. Hagar was able to live in the security of her son's home and
see his children and witness the birth of a nation.

There are things we have been given in our lives. Some of those things
were unexpected or brought much turmoil. Yet, do not despair, for

there may be a promise hidden in a hopeless situation – a precious pearl hidden within a dirty clam, covered in the mud of a dirty sea.

If you are placed in a position in life which you never desired, or if you feel trapped by your circumstances and hopeless of ever being set free, there is a pearl of promise even within your circumstance.

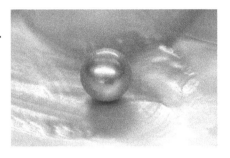

The Journey of a Pearl

The birth of a pearl is a miraculous event! Live oysters below the surface of the sea grow pearls. Gemstones must be cut and polished to bring out their beauty, but  pearls need no such treatment to reveal their loveliness. They are born from oysters complete with a shimmering iridescence, luster and soft inner glow unlike any other gem on Earth.

A natural pearl begins its life as a foreign object, such as a parasite or piece of shell that accidentally lodges itself in an oyster's soft inner body where it cannot be expelled. To ease this irritant, the oyster's body takes defensive action. The oyster begins to secrete a smooth, hard crystalline substance around the irritant in order to protect itself.

This substance is called "nacre." As long as the irritant remains within its body, the oyster will continue to secrete nacre around it, layer upon layer. Over time, the irritant will be completely encased by the silky crystalline coatings, and the result, ultimately, is the lovely and lustrous gem called a **pearl**. https://www.wixonjewelers.com/education/pearls/how-pearls-are-formed/

Personal Reflection

Although you may not see it hidden beneath the darkness and dirt of your life, it is there, precious and beautiful, created as a priceless gem

Do not lose hope in the promise upon your life, for God has sacrificed all for its value.

45Again, the Kingdom of Heaven is like a merchant on the lookout for choice pearls. 46When he discovered a pearl of great value, he sold everything he owned and bought it! Matthew 13:45-46

Do not give in to despair and "cast off" what God has for you. Do not discard the pearl of promise for things and people who do not see it. Give it to God who can bring the promise to life.

Do not give what is holy to the dogs; nor cast your pearls before swine, lest they trample them under their feet, and turn and tear you in pieces. Matthew 7:6

Do not feel hopeless in the positions you have been placed, for God is with you and is able to preserve you and bless you, better and stronger, for His glory.

8We are pressed on every side by troubles, but we are not crushed. We are perplexed, but not driven to despair. 9We are hunted down, but never abandoned by God. We get knocked down, but we are not destroyed. 2 Corinthians 4:8-9

"A pearl is a beautiful thing that is produced by an injured life. It is the tear that results from the injury of the oyster. The treasure of our being in this world is also produced by an injured life. If we had not been wounded, if we had not been injured, then we will not produce the pearl."

– Stephen Hoeller, American Author and Scholar

Chapter 14
You promised me

David was the father of Solomon (whose mother was Bathsheba, the widow of Uriah). Matthew 1:6b

Bathsheba, like Hagar, was a victim of other people's sins and manipulations. She became a widow, an adulterer, and a mother who knows the deep pain of losing a child (there is no name for this). She was used as an object of lust, a pawn for cover-up, and a receptacle for sin, yet God did not overlook Bathsheba. For He gave her a promise and she hung onto it until it was realized.

After the prophet "outed" David and God pronounced his judgment, Bathsheba gave birth to a son who later dies despite David's earnest fasting and praying. The Bible does not comment on how Bathsheba felt or reacted, but we can only imagine the depth of her grief and despair.

David and Bathsheba conceive again and give birth to Solomon. Solomon is the seventh son of David and by law, is not supposed to inherit the kingdom, but God chose Solomon and favored him.

> *Then David comforted Bathsheba, his wife, and slept with her. She became pregnant and gave birth to a son, and David named him Solomon. The Lord loved the child and sent word through Nathan the prophet that they should name him Jedidiah* (which means "beloved of the Lord"), *as the Lord had commanded.*
>
> *Genesis 12:24*

Yet because of David's sin, we know that it set off a chain of reactions that caused his eldest son to rape his sister, one son to murder another and attempt to overthrow David's kingdom.

Despite these horrible circumstances, God's calling on Solomon's life remained.

When David became old and near death, his other son, Adonijah, sought to take over his father's kingdom but Nathan the prophet and the priest did not support him. The same prophet who proclaimed God's judgment over David, told Bathsheba about the plot and advised her to go into King David and remind him of God's promise over Solomon.

> *15So Bathsheba went into the king's bedroom. (He was very old now, and Abishag was taking care of him.) 16Bathsheba bowed down before the king.*
>
> *"What can I do for you?" he asked her.*
>
> *17She replied, "My lord, you made a vow before the Lord your God when you said to me, 'Your son Solomon will surely be the next king and will sit on my throne.'*
>
> *18But instead, Adonijah has made himself king, and my lord the king does not even know about it. 19He has sacrificed many cattle, fattened calves, and sheep, and he has invited all the king's sons to attend the celebration. He also invited Abiathar the priest and Joab, the commander of the army. But he did not invite your servant Solomon.*
>
> *20And now, my lord the king, all Israel is waiting for you to announce who will become king after you. 21If you do not act, my son Solomon and I will be treated as criminals as soon as my lord the king has died."*
>
> *1 Kings 1:15-21*

David promised Bathsheba that Solomon would be the one to inherit the throne. Although David promised, this promise was from God.

For even the prophet of God recognized the promise for Solomon even though the child was birthed from the soil of death and deceit. Likewise, regardless of the circumstances of our births, our lives are marked by His promise and purpose.

Bathsheba fought for her son. She stood on the promise she was given. She did not let go of the only answer to the question as to why she went through what she went through. She did not discard the one thing that could bring closure to her suffering. Although she was blind to many things, she trusted God who promised her.

> [28]*King David responded, "Call Bathsheba!" So, she came back in and stood before the king. [29]And the king repeated his vow: "As surely as the Lord lives, who has rescued me from every danger, [30]your son Solomon will be the next king and will sit on my throne this very day, just as I vowed to you before the Lord, the God of Israel."*
>
> [31]*Then Bathsheba bowed down with her face to the ground before the king and exclaimed, "May my lord King David live forever!"*
>
> *1 King 1:28-31*

I will lead the blind by a way they do not know, In paths they do not know I will guide them I will make darkness into light before them And rugged places into plains These are the things I will do, And I will not leave them undone. Isaiah 42:1

Bathsheba witnessed her son become king. Solomon was considered one of the greatest kings of Israel and brought peace to the nation. This would have happened whether she believed or not, but by keeping her faith in the will of God, Bathsheba survived and saw the blessing that came from her pain. She was blessed to become the Queen Mother, the highest position in the nation for a woman.

Personal Reflection

God knows the end from the beginning. His plans do not change with our failures, successes, or the sin of our lives. What role we play in the story is up to our faith and trust in God.

We must not allow the painful circumstances of our lives, to cause us to dismiss the promises of God.

Even if those promises are hidden in the places where death dwells:

A Shunamite woman was content with not being able to have children, until the man of God prophesied a son. This son grew up only to die in her arms. Without delay, she placed her dead son on the bed of the prophet. She ran and grabbed the feet of that prophet and demanded an account for the promise spoken unto her life.

Then she said, "Did I ask you for a son, my lord? And didn't I say, 'Don't deceive me and get my hopes up'?" 2 Kings 4:28

The prophet brought her son back to life.

36 Then Elisha summoned Gehazi. "Call the child's mother!" he said. And when she came in, Elisha said, "Here, take your son!" 37 She fell at his feet and bowed before him, overwhelmed with gratitude.

2 Kings 4:36-37

Even if those promises are hidden in the places where shame dwells

A woman met Jesus at the well when coming at noon for her water. She was thirsty but more than just water. Yet, she had satisfied her thirst with sexual relationships that left her dry and alone at a well. The well was where she obtained her daily water, but it was her place of shame because she could only go there when no one else would be there to judge her and looked down upon her. Yet, at this place of shame, she found her promise in the hope of Jesus.

13 Jesus replied, "Anyone who drinks this water will soon become thirsty again. 14 But those who drink the water I give will never be thirsty again. It becomes a fresh, bubbling spring within them, giving them eternal life." [15]*"Please, sir," the woman said, "give me this water! Then I'll never be thirsty again, and I won't have to come here to get water."*

John 4:13-15

He took her water and bore her shame and in exchange, she and her village received a water that would never run dry and leave them thirsty again.

[28]*The woman left her water jar beside the well and ran back to the village, telling everyone,* [29]*"Come and see a man who told me everything I ever did! Could he possibly be the Messiah?"*

* * *

[39]*Many Samaritans from the village believed in Jesus because the woman had said, "He told me everything I ever did!"*

John 4:28-29, 39

Even if those promises are hidden in the chains of addiction, disease, or stolen dreams.

Your promise lives beneath the rubble of it all. It is waiting for God to unearth at the right time for His glory and your salvation.

I will lead the blind by a way they do not know, In paths they do not know I will guide them I will make darkness into light before them And rugged places into plains These are the things I will do, And I will not leave them undone. Isaiah 42:1

Prayer

Lord, Jesus, I trust You and believe that You will never leave or forsake me. When I am alone, I know that You are my comfort and my strength. Although I have suffered with pain and disease, I believe that You are my healer. Despite the prison of my circumstances, I declare, that in You, I am free.

Lord, I believe but please help my unbelief. Help me to see beyond my circumstances and problems. Lord, open my eyes to see that Your promise remains. Give me wisdom to trust Your will for my life even when I feel helpless and cast aside.

Teach me to be still and wait for You. Teach me to acknowledge You in all of my decisions and actions. Teach me to hold on to Your word and the truth it declares. Lord, teach me to fight for the promise on my life and not cast it away.

Jesus, I give You the dirt and darkness in my life, knowing that it will become a priceless pearl in Your hands.

In Jesus' name. Amen

Section 5
Who do you believe?

"If you want to see miracles, you have to believe before seeing."

– Jason Frenn

Chapter 15
Ladder of Faith

Faith is expressed at many different levels and forms. Some struggle at almost every point, constantly vacillating between trust and despair. Others push through the moments of doubt, showing no sign of disbelief. Then there are those of us when approaching that ladder of faith, choose the safest and the lowest step- so just in case we fall, the pain at the end will not be so great.

It is the latter that I believe most of us today find ourselves. I call it safe faith where we profess a belief in the impossible but expect a practical outcome with a practical explanation.

A safe faith is the knowledge that God can do the impossible, but we expect what's possible for our life. Of course, this is not an indictment on God but more of a reflection of how we see ourselves and possibly how we believe God sees us.

In silence, we dream about the "*if only*" outcomes, but really expect the "*possible*" or "*likely*" outcomes. Anything greater seems to be reserved for those of greater faith, greater ministries, or just greater everything!

However, our limited expectations have nothing to do with a limitless God who honors His word above His name (*Psalms 138:2*).

God is not a man, that he should lie; neither the son of man, that he should repent: hath he said, and shall he not do it? or hath he spoken, and shall he not make it good? Numbers 23:19

The truth is God's will is **for** us. It is not against us. His will is for our good and not evil. He wants to give us good gifts and give us the desires of our hearts. Yet I believe our faith falters when what we believe for doesn't seem to happen or even the opposite seems to happen. We struggle with the unspoken question of whether God is faulty in His promises or whether we are faulty in our faith?

As believing mothers, we commit our children to the Lord. We may pray chapter and verse of God's promises over their lives. We ask for wisdom and discernment with a vision for what they will need in order to have a firm foundation in the Lord.

As parents, our desires for our children are only good. We expect only good for them. We wish good for them and pray good for them.

We seek those opportunities that will build up that which is good and shut down those things that are not good for them, all because we love them and wanted the best for them. That sometimes means we say yes to what they want or desire. It also means saying no when we believe it would be detrimental to their development and future.

My son loved martial arts and would watch movies or documentaries about the art form continually. One movie, in particular, was very popular for its characters, amazing fight scenes, and humor.

Overall, it was a very good and entertaining film, yet for a young eight-year-old boy, some of the content was beyond his age and maturity. For this, he was not allowed to watch the movie.

To my son, I was being unfair. All the other kids were able to watch it as much as they wanted. He couldn't understand why I was being so mean.

He would ask, "What did I do wrong?" or "Why are you punishing me?" "Why are you overreacting?"

Sound familiar? We all have approached God the same way when our requests, even when prayed in faith, are not answered the way we want. It seems unfair as if God is against us. It seems to contradict His word or what He promises when He says, "Ask and it shall be given."

The truth is that even when God's answers are not in line with our specific requests, it is not because He is against us. It is actually because He is for us.

Like a parent, God our Father knows what we need and what we don't. He knows when we can handle something and when we cannot. Moreover, the will of God is beyond our understanding and there are many questions that will not be answered until later or even when we are with the Lord in Heaven.

Yet know this: His will is righteous and His will towards us is righteous…in all things.

The key is to trust the character of God even when the path of faith is cluttered with things that seem to contradict what we are praying for.

Zacharias was a man who had to grapple with clutter.

Zacharias

> [5]*When Herod was king of Judea, there was a Jewish priest named Zacharias. He was a member of the priestly order of Abijah, and his wife, Elizabeth, was also from the priestly line of Aaron.* [6]*Zacharias and Elizabeth were righteous in God's eyes, careful to obey all of the Lord's commandments and regulations.* [7]*They had no children because Elizabeth was unable to conceive, and they were both very old.*

> *Luke 1:5-7*

Zacharias was a priest of the temple of God in the time right before the birth of Jesus. The Bible states that Zacharias and his wife, Elisabeth, were righteous people and dedicated their lives to God. Yet, this couple lacked one important thing, children. Elisabeth was unable to conceive, and she and Zacharias were too old to give it another thought.

Is there something you always wanted in your life, but it never happens?

Have you given up on it because you are too old, too busy, too ill, or too _____(*fill in the blank*)?

Can you relate to Zacharias?

You have remained faithful in serving the Lord and dedicating your life to Him, but have reconciled that those dreams or desires of your heart were not meant for you?

It is not that you blame God, or that you carry anger or sadness, but you figured it wasn't for you and you let it go long ago.

This is the address where Zacharias and Elisabeth lived. They still served, still trusted, still dedicated their lives to their God but had to let go of that one hope of having a child.

"I have so much to be thankful for. Look what God has done for us over the years. I may not have all I wanted, but oh how the Lord has blessed and protected. I trust His will."

You or I may not have spoken these exact words, but we have said or heard some form of this in our lives. We are so thankful for all of God's blessings in our lives. We look back over the years and see His hand at every turn, protecting, answering, keeping, and positioning us for the next step, the next blessing. Yet many of us have hopes, even dreams, which have not been realized and after so long, we have reconciled that those dreams or hopes are not God's will for us.

Truth be told, this may be true. Yet, what happens when a dream is awakened, or we hear the lock to that closed door click open?

Zacharias and Elisabeth were confronted with this unexpected event.

> *[11]While Zacharias was in the sanctuary, an angel of the Lord appeared to him, standing to the right of the incense altar. [12]Zacharias was shaken and overwhelmed with fear when he saw him. [13]But the angel said, "Don't be afraid, Zacharias! God has heard your prayer. Your wife, Elizabeth, will give you a son, and you are to name him John."*
>
> *Luke 1:11-13*

How does one respond after so long a time? Some may retreat and reject the possibility, afraid of what appears to be false hope (*2 Kings 2:14-17*). Others may appear crazy, pushing all common sense aside to grab a hold of their last chance for hope (*Mark 5:25-34*). Yet there are those who respond somewhere in between, not rejecting but not expecting either. These can actually co-exist, and this is where Zacharias is positioned.

Zacharias said to the angel, "How can I be sure this will happen? I'm an old man now, and my wife is also well along in years." Luke 1:18

This is the safest ladder of faith that many of us stand. We do not reject the idea of a limitless God for whom nothing is impossible. This is, indeed, the Word of God. Yet, we may not expect the impossible for ourselves. We are ok with the realistic and the practical, for this is a safe place to dwell where we can still see the floor beneath us, adjusting our position on the ladder of faith with an explanation that makes sense.

This is what Abraham did when God promised that he would be the father of many nations through his elderly and barren wife Sarah. After eleven years of waiting, Abraham and Sarah, his wife, decided to turn the impossible into something reasonable. He fathered a son with another woman who was fertile (*Genesis 16:1-4*). He chose a safe place on his ladder of faith from which he retained control. Abraham never turned his back on God, nor did he stop believing in God's promise, but he, like all of us, placed his own limitations on a limitless God. He put God in a box of his making. This was not what God intended (*Genesis 17:15-19*). God does the impossible, for He specializes in it! He is limitless!

[13] Then the Lord said to Abraham, "Why did Sarah laugh? Why did she say, 'Can an old woman like me have a baby?' [14] Is anything too hard for the Lord? I will return about this time next year, and Sarah will have a son."
Genesis 18:13-14

On which step of the ladder of faith have you found yourself in life?

Can you identify times or areas in your life when your faith exemplified one of the listed levels of faith?

Utter disbelief?

Desperate, open faith?

Safe, reasonable faith?

A Divine Intersection

> *Zacharias said to the angel, "How can I be sure this will happen? I'm an old man now, and my wife is also well along in years." Then the angel said, "I am Gabriel! I stand in the very presence of God. It was he who sent me to bring you this good news! But now, since you didn't believe what I said, you will be silent and unable to speak until the child is born. For my words will certainly be fulfilled at the proper time."*
>
> *Luke 1:18*

Zacharias was not expecting this revelation and his response reflected his doubt in this miraculous possibility. He was comfortable on his ladder of faith where his hope was safe with what is reasonable and predictable. The possibility of having a child at this stage of life was beyond what he could believe or hope.

This is not to criticize him for his disbelief or his doubt because such doubt is common to all of us, yet we would not necessarily expect it from someone like Zacharias.

He was a dedicated servant of God.

He was obedient to God's commands and law.

He was of advanced age and experience.

Yet, he stopped believing in the impossible.

How many of us who have dedicated ourselves to God and his kingdom work can identify with Zacharias if we are truly honest? How many dreams and hopes have we placed on the top shelf as a token of another time and season?

However, God does not forget. Our hopes and desires are ever burning on the altar of God. The Bible says in Psalms that the Lord is mindful of us and considers us. He hears us and provides for us. He keeps His promises.

> [13]*The Lord always keeps His promises; He is gracious in all He does.* [14]*The Lord helps the fallen and lifts those bent beneath their loads.* [15]*The eyes of all look to you in hope; you give them their food as they need it.*
>
> [16]*When You open Your hand, You satisfy the hunger and thirst of every living thing.* [17]*The Lord is righteous in everything He does; He is filled with kindness.*
>
> [18]*The Lord is close to all who call on Him, yes, to all who call on Him in truth.* [19] *He grants the desires of those who fear Him; He hears their cries for help and rescues them.* [20]*The Lord protects all those who love Him, but He destroys the wicked.*
>
> *Psalms 145:13–20*

Yet, some may respond that they have prayed continually for certain things in life yet at the end of their days, those prayers were not granted according to what they asked. Others may argue that not all of our desires or prayer requests will be answered "yes" by God for it is according to His Sovereign will. The response to both of these statements is "true."

Not all of our prayer requests, no matter how long we pray, will be answered in the way we have prayed or granted in the manner we requested. Even Paul acknowledges that he prayed three times for a "thorn in his side" to be removed, a chronic affliction to be healed. Yet God refused to heal him in order to keep him humble and grounded.

Does this mean that God did not care that Paul suffered the affliction or that he was in pain? Does this mean that God does not care that we suffer from afflictions, disabilities, or remain unmarried or childless? The answer is no. God does care. In fact, He delights in giving His children the kingdom!

So don't be afraid, little flock. For it gives your Father great happiness to give you the Kingdom. Luke 12:32

God's will to use Paul through His anointed power, revelation, and strength was greater than Paul's need to be healed of the "thorn." In fact, the "thorn" afforded Paul greater power, greater revelation, and greater strength. The "thorn" kept Paul's focus on God and his complete dependence on Him for all things. Paul stopped praying after three times, understanding that his burden and prayers for the church and for the lost was greater than his own burden and affliction. He aligned his will with that of the Father. His prayers reflected the will of the Lord and in all this, he was content (*Philippians 4:11-13*).

Even our Lord, when at his human breaking point, prayed that he would not have to go through what he would have to endure in order to save mankind. Yet, he conceded to the will of the Father, when He said, "nevertheless not my will but Thine be done." The love of God is so beyond measure that His will was to sacrifice His only begotten son to save the world. Jesus conceded His will to the will of God acknowledging that it was for this reason He came (*Luke 22:42*).

So, yes, we all have prayers or desires for which God's answer may be "no." Since God is for us (*Romans 8:31*), loves us (*Romans 5:8*), and His plans for us are good (*Jeremiah 29:11*), we must trust His will for our lives and submit our will to the His greater will, for His will is good (*Romans 8:23*).

Personal Reflection

We should trust the will of God in our lives because God knows all things, past, present, and future. Even a "no" or "wait" from God could be the closed door needed to move us in a direction we otherwise would not have chosen. It's in this direction, that we find freedom, joy, purpose we never thought possible and never could have imagined if we had actually received what we wanted or moved in a direction of our choosing.

We all can think of examples, when we sought after things for which we could not wait for God to provide. After seeking it for ourselves, we found ourselves more burdened, broken, and less fulfilled than before.

We do not even have to look far in the Bible when we consider Abraham who could not wait on God. Abraham conceived a son, not of his wife. This was the son to whom Abraham was forced to become a "dead beat" dad and the son who would subsequently birth a nation that still, today, fights for its birthright.

So, trust God even if your answer is a resounding "no". For in the "no" resides a "yes" to something tailor-made just for you and something that you could never have dreamed or imagined for yourself.

Trust.

Chapter 16
A Divine Intersection
– When your will and
God's will collide

Zacharias had resolved that he and his wife, Elisabeth, would remain barren. This is evident from his response to the angel. Yet, God did not forget Zacharias' prayer, and, in His time, He granted this elderly, faithful couple their prayer request. Yet, one can scarcely blame Zacharias for his doubt and disbelief.

And Zacharias said unto the angel, "Whereby shall I know this?" for I am an old man, and my wife well stricken in years. Luke 1:18

Or if he were speaking today,

"After so many years? Now? How in the world can this happen? I must be dreaming."

Yet Zacharias was not dreaming. God's will which was ordained before time locked into Zacharias's will for a child and the miracle of John the Baptist was born. It did not occur when Zacharias and Elizabeth wanted or expected it. It did not even occur how they expected it. One could even imagine that their miracle son was nothing like what they thought he would be.

'He lives in the wilderness, wears camel skins, and eats grasshoppers! He has become a religious fanatic who looks nothing like the priestly lineage of his father.'

Yet it happened and in such a way where only God could get the glory. So why would God choose them and answer their prayer now when they are too old?

They were not the only couple left barren and desirous of a child. Zacharias was not the only priest who faithfully served God and lived a righteous life. Yet God chose Zacharias and Elisabeth on purpose, for His purpose.

When our prayers and heart's desire collide with God's purpose, miracles happen! The miracle may not look like what you expected nor come in the package you imagined. Yet it is a miracle because God turned your prayer into His purpose, a purpose far greater than your prayer alone could have ever conceived.

Zacharias and Elisabeth had pictured having a son at the age of most young married couples, when they had the energy and vitality to raise a child. He imagined his son following the same calling of the Levitical priesthood, dedicating his life to service and sacrifice. Yet, the child they imagined in their prayers, looked nothing like the bold outspoken John the Baptist, who lived in the wild, eating locusts and honey and proclaiming the way of the Lord through repentance next to a river. Nor did they imagine that his life would be sacrificed at the chopping block of Herod the King. Yet, John the Baptist was all that they had prayed for and more, for his life and calling were ordained long before their time.

Can you look at your life and see where your prayers intersected with the will of God?

What was the outcome of those prayers? Was it what you imagined or pictured?

The truth is God has designed us for purpose, for His purpose. We are not here by accident or as an afterthought. Our purpose is to ultimately glorify God and to spread the knowledge of Him to a lost and broken world. For God loves the world to such a degree, that He gave Himself as a ransom for us in the person of Jesus Christ (*John 3:16*).

Yet, His plan has always been that you and I would be a necessary part of His Divine plan. This is why it is possible that our lives, which are full of ups and downs, mistakes and triumphs, can still be used for God's glory. For regardless of where we find ourselves in life, we are positioned for purpose. So, remember and hear it again: All things work together for good for those who love Him and are called according to His purpose.

If we truly believe this, then we can live our lives with eternal hope in the impossible because we trust the purpose of God. It keeps our faith open to the impossible and properly positioned when God's purpose intersects with our hopes and desires. It keeps us open to what God can do. Yet we can remain at peace if the "*when's?*" and the "*if's?*" go unanswered even after so much time has passed, and many other things have occurred.

What about the lady with a bleeding condition that lasted 12 years after many doctor visits and failed treatments? She remained open to the impossible and kept climbing that ladder of faith despite the number of times she may have asked herself "when?" or "if?"

So, when she came across Jesus, she jumped at the chance to grab a hold of the single answer to her prayer. She was by no means the only one reaching out to touch Jesus, but her earnest prayer aligned with His desire and the result was that she was healed after twelve years. Furthermore, for the rest of history, the world is blessed by her testimony.

What about the three Hebrew boys who were to be burned alive for remaining faithful to their God while living in a sinful world? They knew God could save them but whether He did or did not, they would not reject Him. He, in fact, did save them, and the result was that the same evil King that sent them to be burned alive ended up worshipping their God as the one true God!

Our loving and generous God will honor even the prayers that seem to benefit only ourselves. Hezekiah was one of the few righteous kings of Judah who honored God and made the nation of Judah to do the same. He became deathly ill, but God heard his cry and granted him fifteen additional years of life.

You see for the woman, the Hebrew boys, and King Hezekiah their prayers were desperate and sincere. They trusted that their God could answer them. For some the answer took a long time, for others it actually arrived late, and for one, it was just in time. They never rejected the possibility of the impossible even if the answer was to be "no" in the end.

Yet what if our faith is not open? What if we question or reject the reality of God's plans for us? What if Abraham rejected God's promise to grant him a son through Sarah and focused on raising Ishmael as his chosen son for a future nation? What if the lady with an issue of blood talked herself out of fighting through a crowd just to touch Jesus because "why should this time be any different than the rest?" What if the Hebrew boys decided to kneel in allegiance to King Nebuchadnezzar minutes before they were pushed into the furnace, because God had not yet shown up? There are no answers to these alternate scenarios, but one can imagine the consequences in the lives of these individuals and that of countless generations to come, including our own.

Yet in the case of Zacharias, we have an answer. In order to protect the miraculous birth and purpose of John the Baptist, God prevented Zacharias who originally prayed for a child from then aborting his prayer from coming to life through disbelief.

¹⁹Then the angel said, "I am Gabriel! I stand in the very presence of God. It was he who sent me to bring you this good news! ²⁰But now, since you didn't believe what I said, you will be silent and unable to speak until the child is born. For my words will certainly be fulfilled at the proper time."

Luke 1:19-20

⁵⁷When it was time for Elizabeth's baby to be born, she gave birth to a son. ⁵⁸And when her neighbors and relatives heard that the Lord had been very merciful to her, everyone rejoiced with her.

⁵⁹When the baby was eight days old, they all came for the circumcision ceremony. They wanted to name him Zechariah, after his father. ⁶⁰But Elizabeth said, "No! His name is John!"

⁶¹"What?" they exclaimed. "There is no one in all your family by that name." ⁶²So they used gestures to ask the baby's father what he wanted to name him. ⁶³He motioned for a writing tablet, and to everyone's surprise he wrote, "His name is John." ⁶⁴Instantly Zechariah could speak again, and he began praising God.

⁶⁵Awe fell upon the whole neighborhood, and the news of what had happened spread throughout the Judean hills. ⁶⁶Everyone who heard about it reflected on these events and asked, "What will this child turn out to be?" For the hand of the Lord was surely upon him in a special way.

Luke 1:57-66

The Bible says that life and death are in the power of the tongue and they that love to talk will eat the fruit of it (*Proverbs 18:21*). In other words, the words we say have power. We can speak life, encouragement, hope, and faith into existence just by speaking words that affirm them. We can also speak death, doubt, despair, and fear into existence just by speaking words that affirm them, as well.

By discounting the spoken word of God, Zacharias had the power to block the answer to his own prayer. He spoke doubt and disbelief and if he had continued to speak such words, his words would have blocked the miraculous conception and life of John the Baptist. God

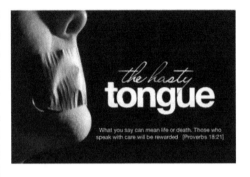

had other plans. So, God shut Zacharias' mouth to prevent him from speaking death before life was ever conceived in Elisabeth.

How many prayers have we blocked or aborted with our words or actions? How many opened doors have we walked past due to fear of the unknown? How many burning bushes have we ignored due to disinterest or disbelief?

Are there prayers from long ago whose answers actually arrived at our doorsteps but we were too busy, fearful, or unbelieving to open and receive them?

You see, Zacharias had settled on a safe position of serving and believing but his faith was capped on a low level, a level that made sense to him. A level from which he rationalized that what he had prayed for was not meant for him and thus was no longer to be prayed or even believed. So, when he found himself at the intersection of God's purpose and a prayer he buried long ago, he prayed a new prayer. He prayed for proof. He prayed for evidence that required no faith. So, God shut his ability to speak his new prayer in order to accomplish the miracle that his original prayer had released.

It wasn't until Zacharias named his son John, the name that God had chosen, that God restored his tongue. When Zacharias demonstrated a belief in the impossible becoming possible, God healed him of his ability to speak and Zacharias was able to praise God for the miracle.

It makes one wonder, if some of the detours or derailments that we have experienced in our lives, was God's way of preventing us from blocking our prayers or delaying His purpose. Only God knows but one thing we can definitely learn from Zacharias and the other heroes of faith is to never stop believing in a limitless and timeless God. For at the right time and right place, we may find ourselves at a divine intersection. We must be ready with a faith and belief in the impossible becoming possible – no matter how long it has been, how far beyond reality it seems, and no matter what has occurred that would seem to disqualify us from receiving.

> *Who against hope believed in hope, that he might become the father of many nations, according to that which was spoken, So shall thy seed be. [19]And being not weak in faith, he considered not his own body now dead, when he was about an hundred years old, neither yet the deadness of Sarah's womb: [20]Abraham never wavered in believing God's promise. In fact, his faith grew stronger, and in this he brought glory to God. [21]He was fully convinced that God is able to do whatever he promises. [22]And because of Abraham's faith, God counted him as righteous. [23]And when God counted him as righteous, it wasn't just for Abraham's benefit. It was recorded [24]for our benefit, too, assuring us that God will also count us as righteous if we believe in him, the one who raised Jesus our Lord from the dead.*

> *Romans 4:18-24*

And it is impossible to please God without faith. Anyone who wants to come to him must believe that God exists and that he rewards those who sincerely seek him. Hebrews 11:6

> *This is what the Lord says:*

> *"At just the right time, I will respond to you.*

> *On the day of salvation, I will help you.*

I will protect you and give you to the people as my covenant with them.

Through you I will reestablish the land of Israel and assign it to its own people again."

Isaiah 49:9

Personal Reflection

"The climb is tough, but the view from the top is worth it." – Anonymous

Maybe you have overlooked or dismissed opportunities for miracles in your life or maybe you did not even recognize the ones that came along. We may miss our answer, our miracle, because we are looking for "*it*."

"*It*" is the answer we have already pictured in our minds. "*It*" is pre-packaged and dressed up, walking and talking as we envision it. Yet God's answer often looks very different than what we picture. God's answer may not fit the picture that we have in our minds. We might reject or dismiss God's answer or miracle standing right before our eyes. Furthermore, we may find ourselves going after "its" that look like answered prayers from a distance. Yet up close, they are far from miracles and often the substance of our worst nightmares!

On some level, you may feel unworthy to receive what you have been praying and believing for from God. Daresay, you may even resent or distrust God for what appears to be an unanswered prayer or worse, an "*it*" answer which has left you unfulfilled or damaged.

Regardless of where your faith stands, God remains faithful to His holy will which includes His will for you. He is known for turning His attention to His beloved in due season and in due time, for He never forgets and never retracts His promises.

He remains at the top of your ladder of faith with all the answers and miracles. The question is, can you step back on your ladder of faith and continue to move up step by step?

The key to climbing a ladder is to keep looking up to where you want to land. For it is when you look down at the ground and see how far you are from the ground, that fear and doubt rise up to slow you down, to make you stop, or to return down to a place of safety and comfort. Or it is when you look at your feet, carefully watching how each foot securely plants itself on each rung, that you increasingly depend on yourself for guidance and provision and look to your own strength to reach your destination.

So, it is with our faith.

The key to never stop believing and trusting God for your miracle is to never take your eyes off Him.

Then if my people who are called by my name will humble themselves and pray and seek my face and turn from their wicked ways, I will hear from heaven and will forgive their sins and restore their land. 2 Chronicles 7:14

Look straight ahead, and fix your eyes on what lies before you.

Mark out a straight path for your feet; stay on the safe path.

Don't get sidetracked; keep your feet from following evil.

Proverbs 4:25

But seek first the kingdom of God and His righteousness, and all these things shall be added to you. Matthew 6:33

It is Jesus our Lord who has all power in heaven and earth. He is not bound by the limits of birth and death, earth and sky, years or seconds. All of creation is under his authority and power. There is *nothing* impossible with Him.

So, the ladder of faith is not for Him, it is for you. He wants you to take steps toward Him even when you are leaving the ground of comfort and safety with nothing but His promises to hang onto. He wants you to keep your eyes of faith set on Him, even when you cannot see the next rung of the ladder to step upon. Trust that it is there, and step.

For when we let go of what we stand on and what we see and focus only on who God is, we will see Him more clearly the closer we get to Him. We will see His character and His heart and know that we can trust Him for the answer at His timing and for His purpose.

So, take a *step*, then take *another step* and *another step*, and never stop believing in the Lord God Almighty.

Chapter 17
The Faith of Women and Children

Women are naturally creatures of faith. From the moment a little girl can dream, we fantasize about our lives as wives, mothers, professionals, or ballerinas. We role-play with our dolls and stuffed animals, acting out our fantasies and daydreams. We sing with our hairbrushes the songs we envision singing before thousands.

As we grow into women, we continue to believe in things and people even in the face of disappointment and let-downs.

Whether in our homes, schools, or work, women are naturally good at having faith and the examples are endless.

> *The teacher who spends her own money on educational resources even though she is underpaid because she believes in her students' potential.*

> *The executive who is twice overlooked for a promotion but works extra-long hours to complete the big project because she still believes that her hard work will pay off.*

> *The wife who works two jobs to support her husband while he starts his own business because she believes in his dream and his potential.*

This is not to say that men and boys do not have faith or belief in the same things. In fact, there are many examples of men of great faith who have sacrificed all for what they believe such as Martin Luther King, Mahatma Gandhi, Abraham Lincoln, Billy Graham, and the countless men and boys that we encounter every day who inspire us because of their faith. Let's not forget to mention the great men listed in the chapter of faith in Chapter 12 of Hebrews such as Abraham, Gideon, Noah, and Samson, to name a few.

However, when we look a little closer at history and that of our own, the journey to faith is often much shorter for women. We by no means hold the position for great faith but we often get there first. We are often the first to believe without seeing, first to move despite our fears, first to support and love the underdog, and the first one to defend another without thought of self.

The Faith of a Mother

This is no more evident than the faith of a mother. A mother will sacrifice everything for the welfare and care of her child. Even before birth, a mother already has hopes and dreams about their child and prepares for his or her arrival. This may not appear like faith, but it is faith in a life that is yet to be born. It is a faith that causes a mother to buy clothes for someone not yet here or decorate a room when there is no one there to sleep in it. For faith is more than a belief, it is the action behind that belief that makes it true faith (*Hebrew 2:14*).

After a child is born, the faith of a mother grows. She worries, prays, and works to create a safe and loving home for her child. She does this not only because she loves the child but because of a faith in the life and potential of her child. She must make sure her baby has all that it needs to survive and to thrive…because she has faith in what her child can become.

It is this same faith that keeps a mother on her knees praying when the dreams she has for her child seem to disappear in the wake of life's circumstances. It is this faith that keeps a mother working, sacrificing, and giving when the dreams she carried for her child become more like nightmares. It is this faith, which allows a mother to do it all again and again for each new child, including the ones she did not birth.

However, this does not mean that such faith is exclusive to women or mothers, nor does it mean that all who have children show such love or faith. Yet the idea or concept of motherhood is often defined by an undying love, support, and faith in her children.

The Bible says that faith is the substance of things hoped for and the evidence of things not seen (*Hebrews 11:1*). Thus, the faith of mothers is a great example of a hope that begins long before the evidence of her belief and hard work is ever visualized.

Using this example, there are three aspects of such faith:

1. Does not stop believing;
2. Sacrificial; and
3. Blind to contradiction.

As previously stated, such faith is not exclusive to just women. When we think of the great people of faith in the Bible, we think of the faith of Abraham. God promised that an elderly childless Abraham would not only have children but would become the Father of nations. God promised that his seed would dwell in a land that had been occupied by others for centuries.

> *¹When Abram was ninety-nine years old, the Lord appeared to him and said, "I am El-Shaddai—'God Almighty.' Serve me faithfully and live a blameless life. ²I will make a covenant with you, by which I will guarantee to give you countless descendants."*
>
> *³At this, Abram fell face down on the ground. Then God said to him, ⁴"This is my covenant with you: I will make you the father of a multitude of nations! ⁵What's more, I am changing your name. It will no longer be Abram. Instead, you will be called Abraham, for you will be the father of many nations. ⁶I will make you extremely fruitful. Your descendants will become many nations, and kings will be among them!*
>
> *⁷I will confirm my covenant with you and your descendants after you, from generation to generation. This is the everlasting covenant: I will always be your God and the God of*

*your descendants after you. ⁸And I will give the entire land
of Canaan, where you now live as a foreigner, to you and
your descendants. It will be their possession forever, and I
will be their God."*

Genesis 17:1-8

It is this faith that allowed Abraham to obey God and move to sacrifice his only son, Isaac, because he trusted God's promise that he would be the father of many nations. He did not understand how this could happen, but he trusted God at His word, even if it meant killing the only means by which his promise would be realized. He demonstrated the three aspects of faith.

He never (1) *stopped believing* God no matter the (2) *sacrifice required*.

"Take your son, your only son—yes, Isaac, whom you love so much—and go to the land of Moriah. Go and sacrifice him as a burnt offering on one of the mountains, which I will show you." Genesis 22:2

He believed, despite not understanding. He chose to be (3) *blind to the contradiction* of his circumstance and God's promise.

> *¹⁷By faith Abraham, when he was tried, offered up Isaac:
> and he that received the promises offered up his only begotten
> son, ¹⁸of whom it was said, That in Isaac shall thy seed be
> called: ¹⁹Accounting that God was able to raise him up, even
> from the dead; from whence also he received him in a figure.*

Hebrews 11:17-19

Abraham is rightfully called the father of faith. He trusted God's promise and direction despite being completely blind and ignorant of what that promise would look like or how and when it would come about. His faith in God caused him to move step by step at God's command, not able to see the path beyond where his feet could step.

He and his family moved to a land promised to him by God despite the fact that this Promise Land was inhabited and controlled by other people.

He was given the miracle of fatherhood and trusted God that he would be the father of "many nations" although he never lived to see "the nations."

He was asked to sacrifice the one son in whom the promise dwelt. He moved in obedience although he was unable to control or understand how God could both kill and fulfill without forfeiting his promise.

Abraham had to trust what he could not see. He had to believe God for the promise despite the contradiction of his circumstances.

He had to not only trust that he would be a father to a child of his own, but also a father of a great nation despite the fact that he was old, and his wife was barren.

He had to trust that even with his mistakes and sin, that God would remain faithful to the son of His promise and faithful to the other son born outside of His will.

Abraham is called the father of faith because he never stopped believing God and acted on his belief. He was willing to sacrifice the son of promise despite the contradiction of giving Isaac back to God.

The only other example where we see such faith is the faith of a child. Yet we often overlook the faith of children because we know that they do not know all the facts nor can they really understand them, yet that is exactly what God wants from us. For it is this kind of faith that is considered as the greatest in the Kingdom of God.

> *¹About that time the disciples came to Jesus and asked, "Who is greatest in the Kingdom of Heaven?"*
>
> *²Jesus called a little child to him and put the child among them. ³Then he said, "I tell you the truth, unless you turn from your sins and become like little children, you will never get into the Kingdom of Heaven. ⁴So, anyone who becomes as humble as this little child is the greatest in the Kingdom of Heaven."*
>
> *Matthew 18:1–4*

Faith of Child

There is no greater example of faith than that of little children. The gift of childhood is to believe. A child's mind is open to words, sounds, and sights, which leave an indelible imprint on them for the rest of her life.

There is no other time when we believe in fairy tales, jolly fat men who bring presents for the whole world in one night, and small little fairies that enter our rooms at night and put money under our pillow for our tooth. There is no other time when we can joyfully believe, accept the words of those around us, and respond with a blind faith that what we have been told will surely happen.

When a child is nurtured in a secure, loving environment with love, that childlike faith allows her to be free to explore, create, and rest in her world. She acts without hesitation and trusts without question. The object of such powerful belief is in her parents, the first people she sees, touches, and experiences in human life – the ones she trusts to show her truth and provide safety.

Yet, if a child's life is chaotic, unpredictable where promises are not kept and love is marked by condition and pain, that child becomes isolated, angry, fearful, and unsettled-always searching for a place to land but without provision or support.

For this child, the tooth fairy becomes an abductor, and Santa Claus becomes a hustler, and God does not care or doesn't exist.

Yet, God created us to grow up with love, security, and a faith that expands and deepens throughout life. A faith in our heavenly Father, where we can explore, create, and rest in the world He created for us.

This has been God's plan from creation. Before the fall, Adam and Eve were free from shame, fear, and unbelief. They could run to their Father anytime and then go to explore and populate the world without fear because their Father was always there. He protected. He guided and taught them.

[27]So, God created human beings[a] in his own image. In the image of God, he created them; male and female he created them.

[28]Then God blessed them and said, "Be fruitful and multiply. Fill the earth and govern it. Reign over the fish in the sea, the birds in the sky, and all the animals that scurry along the ground."

Genesis 1:27-28

Mankind was free and empowered to grow in limitless knowledge, create astounding things, and discover the deepest secrets left hidden like treasures in a treasure hunt. One can only imagine a world where man's potential has not been capped and mutated by sin. Where we use 100% of our brain's capacity. Where our imagination and creativity lead us to explore other galaxies and dimensions; where the first, second, and third heavens spoken of in the Bible are as accessible as the playground or a trip to Paris.[6]

One can only imagine, for we can never know such a life on this earth where we have put faith in ourselves instead of God.

The moment Adam and Eve doubted God's goodness and His truth, our world began to shrink, our vision became distorted, and our heart became hardened. It became harder to see God or know Him and easier to see and trust those things we created as our truth.

> [6]*And when the woman saw that the tree was good for food, and that it was pleasant to the eyes, and a tree to be desired to make one wise, she took of the fruit thereof, and did eat, and gave also unto her husband with her; and he did eat. [7]And the eyes of them both were opened, and they knew that they were naked; and they sewed fig leaves together and made themselves aprons.*
>
> *Genesis 3:6-7*

---

6   2 Corinthians 12:1-3.

Close Your Eyes

Then Jesus told him, "You believe because you have seen me. Blessed are those who believe without seeing me." John 20:29

It is interesting that when Satan tempted Eve, he told her that her "eyes shall be opened." He planted a seed of doubt that God was holding something back. This cast a shadow on her world where her faith was replaced by fear.

"If the one who I trusted completely, cannot be trusted, then I must define truth for myself. I must take control of things. I must feel with my hands. I must see it with my eyes. I must make my own path and secure my own way in this world."

Before the fall, Adam and Eve trusted that the herb and the fruit would grow. They trusted that the Garden would remain lush, soft, and secure. They trusted God's command that one tree was not to be eaten without needing further explanation. They trusted that God was who He said He was to them, their loving Father. They trusted without needing to search for an answer to the question of 'what is really true'…until they had to "see" it with their own eyes.

Are there moments in your life when you viewed your circumstances through a lens of faith in God or a lens of pride or fear?

Adam and Eve changed their view. Instead of focusing on God and His provision, they questioned Him and turned their focus to themselves as their own provider and sustainer. The result created a new dimension, an alternate existence marked by evil imaginations, greed, murder, lies, heartache, and suffering. A world where faith sits on a high dusty shelf where most cannot reach because of the clutter of self-indulgence, self-preservation, and self-exaltation.

For the world only feeds the cravings for physical pleasure and self-exaltation which can never satisfy.

A craving for everything we see.

[And when the woman saw that the tree was good for food,]

A craving for our own lusts and desires.

[that it was pleasant to the eyes]

A craving for our self-promotion and independence

[a tree to be desired to make one wise][7]

The objects of our cravings are not from the Father but are from this world. These cravings only lead to death and utter darkness where we hide away from His Presence, unable to truly see the Lord or trust His love and faithfulness.

This is why the enemy works overtime to kill, steal, and destroy any opportunity to "see" God (*John 10:10*).

For if we see Him, we shall believe Him, and if we believe Him, we shall trust Him, and if we trust Him…we will love and obey Him.

If we love and obey Him, all things are possible.

Jesus looked at them intently and said, "Humanly speaking, it is impossible. But with God everything is possible." Matthew 19:26

Satan's desire is that we see with our own eyes through a lens clouded by doubt and fear. For if we look at things with fear and doubt, our vision will be distorted.

We will see lies where there is truth.

We will see despair where there is hope.

We will see loss where there is sacrifice.

We will see punishment where there is chastisement.

We will see problems where there is protection.

We will see restriction where there is freedom.

Personal Reflection

The word says that faith is defined as the *substance of things hoped for, and the evidence of things not seen* (*Hebrew 11:1*).

7   Genesis 3:6; 1 John 2:16

When we look through the lens of faith, we are able to see beyond the natural and see God.

We trust that God is good and all of His plans for us are good. We trust that He does not lie. We trust that He does not change.

We trust that although we may not be able to see it, it already exists because our faith in God is all the evidence we need.

We trust that regardless of the circumstance, God is for us and we can give Him our life and our future, knowing that it will ultimately be right in the end.

"I was so disappointed that I did not get the promotion. I prayed and worked so hard and felt dejected when someone with less experience was chosen. Now, when I look back, I can see where God was keeping me for something else, something better. I am so thankful I did not get that promotion. I can see it would have kept me in a place of stress and chaos. I am so happy now that I see what God had planned for me all along."

"I wanted him so bad. I thought he was the perfect man for me. I fantasized about marriage and family. When he left, I felt like dying. I had no hope of being a wife and mother. I thought something was wrong with me. Thank God, I never married him. I see now what God was keeping me from, things that I was blind to at the time. I praise Him for His grace and mercy. He knew what would happen if we remained together. I am so glad I let God have His way. It was a great hurt that God turned into a hallelujah!"

"I have prayed over my son since we conceived him. I asked that God keep him and protect him. Yet, as a young man, he struggled and chose paths that would lead to his destruction. I was scared and questioned the promises that God gave me over my son. I pictured every horrible alternative. Then God reminded me of His promise many years ago and how He has kept my son. I heard sermons and testimonies of the same and began to speak God's truth and God's word over my son and our family. I chose to speak life and not death. I thanked Him instead of questioning Him, even when what I saw in the natural was the opposite of what I prayed.

God kept His promise. It was not easy. My son stumbled and was bruised along the way, but he was not defeated. God turned what was meant for evil and transformed it into an anointed life and testimony."

"My greatest fear happened. My husband cheated on me. I was blind-sided. I sensed a change in our relationship, but I had no idea that in his heart he had already left me. I have never experienced such pain. My heart was shattered, and I became a shell. It was during this dark time that God became my everything. You see, I had depended on myself and my marriage and kids to find happiness, but through this trial, I learned to depend on Him for everything. God became my husband, my father, my mother, my friend, and my children. When all of my strength and my devices were proven powerless, all I had was Him and He was faithfully there. Now no matter what happens or what happens to me, God is my everything. He is enough!"

Can you choose to close your natural eyes to the circumstances that speak against God's promises? Can you reject the world's definition of truth which only leads to failure, loss, or death? Can you "close your eyes" with a blind faith, stand on the immutable word of God and His promises, and believe that God is for you?

You believe because you have seen me. Blessed are those who believe without seeing me. John 20:29

No matter what has happened, God is sovereign. His will is always good. Whether today, tomorrow, or on the other side of time, His will for you is good. Can you trust Him? Can you trust what you cannot see? Can you trust that He is a good Father who never forsakes, never changes, and never stops loving you?

Like a child, you can run to Him with all of your questions and trust Him for the answers at the right season and stage of your life.

For all of the answers you seek are found in God. Can you wait on His answers? Can you serve and trust Him, until He makes it all good?

In his kindness God called you to share in his eternal glory by means of Christ Jesus. So after you have suffered a little while, he will restore, support, and strengthen you, and he will place you on a firm foundation. 1

Corinthians 5:10

And we know that God causes everything to work together for the good of those who love God and are called according to his purpose for them. Romans 8:28

Chapter 18
The Faith of Mary

And blessed is she that believed for there shall be a performance of those things which were told her from the Lord. Luke 1:45

Six months after Zacharias and Elisabeth conceived John the Baptist, Elisabeth's cousin, Mary, became pregnant. Elisabeth was going to have a son well beyond her childbearing years and young Mary would also know the joy of having a child.

This should have been a time of celebration for both women, their husbands, and their families. This was the case for Elisabeth. Her pregnancy was a miracle. It was literally inconceivable and a source of great joy and celebration for all.

Yet, for Mary, her pregnancy from its beginning was shrouded in confusion, scandal, and sacrifice.

Mary was to be married to a man, named Joseph. It is likely that their families negotiated their union. As a young wife, she was expected to birth children for her husband and become a faithful wife and woman of her community. She would assist her husband in his work as a carpenter and would help to raise their children under the Law of God and Moses. This was her set path. This was the life expected for a young girl. This was to be her state and station in life.

There is not much detail provided about Mary or her personal life. When we look at her story from a distance, we know that she was young, engaged, and lived in a small village town of low reputation. She married a man named Joseph and had several children (*Mark 6:3; Matthew 13:55-56*). Her husband was a carpenter, likely of stone that was abundant in the region. From this perspective, Mary's life would seem normal with nothing interesting or worthy of intrigue.

Yet, it is the story between the story that provides a glimpse into the life of this seemingly average little girl – a glimpse of tenacious faith that would carry her through the most difficult and glorious times of her life.

> [26] *In the sixth month of Elizabeth's pregnancy, God sent the angel Gabriel to Nazareth, a village in Galilee,* [27] *to a virgin named Mary. She was engaged to be married to a man named Joseph, a descendant of King David.* [28] *Gabriel appeared to her and said, "Greetings, favored woman! The Lord is with you!"*
>
> *Luke 1:26-28*

Mary had a secret. A secret for which she might be killed if revealed to the wrong person. For at a time when she should be preparing for marriage and getting excited about the celebrations and well wishes, Mary carried a secret that could end in the destruction of her hopes and dreams.

> [29] *But when she saw him, she was troubled at his saying, and considered what manner of greeting this was. Then the angel said to her,* [30] *"Do not be afraid, Mary, for you have found favor with God.* [31] *And behold, you will conceive in your womb and bring forth a Son and shall call His name Jesus.* [32] *He will be great, and will be called the Son of the Highest; and the Lord God will give Him the throne of His father David.* [33] *And He will reign over the house of Jacob forever, and of His kingdom there will be no end."*
>
> *Luke 1:29-33*

Mary became pregnant, but not by her fiancée, Joseph. If discovered, she could be kicked out of her community to live out her shame with no husband to claim the child. Worse, she could be killed for committing adultery under God's law, not to mention the blasphemy of claiming she is carrying the Son of God.

I am the Lord's servant. May everything you have said about me come true.
Luke 1:38

Despite the danger that her secret carried, Mary was a willing participant. She consented to her situation. She accepted and agreed to it. One could argue that anyone else would not have been so willing if she really understood what was required. Yet, with the faith of a child, she believed God at His word.

Even if we lived in the time of Mary and believed her account of these supernatural events, we still might struggle with her response and her belief.

> *Mary is young and naïve. If she really understood the "cross" she will bear, I am sure she would not be so willing.*

> *Mary probably doesn't know what the angel really meant when he told her that the Holy Ghost would come upon her.*

> *I am not sure I believe this is of God. Why would God do this outside of wedlock and bring such shame? Isn't that against the law? This is of the devil.*

We do not know to what extent Mary really understood the implication of this miracle upon her life when she first encountered the messenger of God. Did she really consider how she was to explain her pregnancy to her parents who were proud to have a virgin daughter? What about Joseph? How could she possibly explain to her fiancée that she was innocent of sexual indiscretion or assault and was actually chosen by God for such a prophetic purpose?

No, we do not know what Mary's thoughts or considerations were when she answered the angel *"May everything you have said about me come true."* Yet, it is not hard to imagine that she had to face these issues and questions as she began to walk the path set before her.

We can only judge Mary by her actions, what she said and what she did, in order to determine who she was and what she believed. For it is her actions that define her as a child of faith who later became a great woman of faith.

It is likely that at her age, Mary had little experience with the highs and lows of life or the struggle between right and wrong. Yet, she chose to believe God at His word and to never let go of his Promise.

In fact, when you compare Mary and her response to God to that of Zacharias, the husband of Elisabeth and the father of John the Baptist, there are marked differences between the two.

Zacharias	Mary
Older married man	Young engaged girl
Life committed to serving God	Life just beginning
Example of Faith and obedience	Example of innocence and naiveté
Needed proof from God	Needed affirmation from God
Spoke against his prayer	Said yes to her promise

Mary was a young girl and inexperienced in life. She was engaged and living with her family. She lived in a small town of no reputation and it can be assumed that her relationship with God was based on the Laws of Moses and traditions of Jewish culture. However, if we peer a little deeper into the scriptures pertaining to Mary, we can see that Mary was possibly seeking for more in her life.

> *26And in the sixth month the angel Gabriel was sent from God unto a city of Galilee, named Nazareth, 27to a virgin espoused to a man whose name was Joseph, of the house of David; and the virgin's name was Mary. 28And the angel came in unto her, and said, "Hail, thou that art highly favoured, the Lord is with thee: blessed art thou among women." 29And when she saw him, she was troubled at his saying, and cast in her mind what manner of salutation this should be. And the angel said unto her, 30"Fear not, Mary: for thou hast found favour with God."*

> *Luke 1:26-30*

Can you imagine experiencing such an event as a little girl? You are alone in your room, playing with your dolls, or singing your favorite tune with your hairbrush microphone and a glorious person appears with this greeting.

This average little girl who was expected to live an average life and do average things was greeted with the same greeting as a King, a High Priest, or someone of great reputation and position. Unlike Zacharias, Mary was greeted with a positive declaration of her identity.

Hail, thou that art highly favoured, the Lord is with thee: blessed art thou among women.

In Merriam-Webster's dictionary, to be favored means to treat with kindness or to prefer by showing support and advantage. In Greek, the word for favor is *charis* which means grace or kindness.[8] This is grace given as a gift or blessing.

So, God entered this little girl's room and announced that she is special, favored, blessed. He essentially stated that she was favored and set apart for special blessing. No wonder she was troubled at this proclamation for the Bible says she was troubled. Why?

Was Mary troubled because she had never considered herself as someone to be favored or as special? Was she troubled because no one treated her as special? What might she have thought of herself since her life was already determined by others – her parents, her fiancée, and her community?

Yet before God could declare the great purpose bestowed upon her, He first had to tell her *who* she was. Unlike Zacharias, she didn't need her fears addressed. She didn't need proof of who was speaking or what was promised. She needed affirmation of her identity.

Have words of affirmation and identity ever been spoken to you?

Do you need affirmation of who you are in God's eyes?

Would you believe it?

All of us as need affirmation of our identity and our value. Yet events

8   https://www.merriam-webster.com/dictionary/favor

in life and consequences of sin have stolen away those priceless declarations, often at a very young age.

Yet God's declaration of who you are and to whom you belong remains the same.

Like Mary, you are blessed and highly favored and if you can fix your faith to that truth, then you can declare, "Lord, I am yours. I believe that I am who You say I am. I trust I will fulfill the purpose you have given me!"

Fixed Faith

What is fixed faith? A fixed faith is one that does not change. No matter the circumstance. No matter the situation. Fixed faith never stops believing.

Mary had fixed faith. From the moment God announced her identity and purpose, she never stopped believing what He declared and promised.

"Behold the maidservant of the Lord! Let it be to me according to your word." And the angel departed from her. Luke 1:3

> *And Mary said: "My soul magnifies the Lord, And my spirit has rejoiced in God my Savior. For He has regarded the lowly state of His maidservant; For behold, henceforth all generations will call me blessed. For He who is mighty has done great things for me."*
>
> *Luke 1:46–49*

The question is how does a young girl with limited life experiences and knowledge, trust God at His word?

The truth is we may never know the how, for all we have are her actions throughout her life and the life of her son.

Actions of a Fixed Faith

Mary had to trust God at His word even in the face of rumors and scandal.

⁴¹And it happened, when Elizabeth heard the greeting of Mary, that the babe leaped in her womb; and Elizabeth was filled with the Holy Spirit. ⁴²Then she spoke out with a loud voice and said, "Blessed are you among women, and blessed is the fruit of your womb! ⁴³But why is this granted to me, that the mother of my Lord should come to me? ⁴⁴For indeed, as soon as the voice of your greeting sounded in my ears, the babe leaped in my womb for joy. ⁴⁵Blessed is she who believed, for there will be a fulfillment of those things which were told her from the Lord."

Luke 1:41-45

Mary had to trust God that Joseph would not change his mind due to the shame he suffered because of her secret.

¹⁸After His mother Mary was betrothed to Joseph, before they came together, she was found with child of the Holy Spirit. ¹⁹Then Joseph her husband, being a just man, and not wanting to make her a public example, was minded to put her away secretly. ²⁰But while he thought about these things, behold, an angel of the Lord appeared to him in a dream, saying, "Joseph, son of David, do not be afraid to take to you Mary your wife, for that which is conceived in her is of the Holy Spirit."...²⁴Then Joseph, being aroused from sleep, did as the angel of the Lord commanded him and took to him his wife, and did not know her till she had brought forth her firstborn Son.

Matthew 1:18-20, 24a

Mary had to trust God when she and her husband were forced to go to another town at the time of her delivery, without lodging or support of family. How does a smelly animal stable in a foreign land as the birthplace for your firstborn son fit in with God's declaration?

¹And it came to pass in those days that a decree went out from Caesar Augustus that all the world should be registered. ²This census first took place while Quirinius was governing Syria. ³So all went to be registered, everyone to his own city.

⁴Joseph also went up from Galilee, out of the city of Nazareth, into Judea, to the city of David, which is called Bethlehem, because he was of the house and lineage of David, ⁵to be registered with Mary, his betrothed wife, who was with child. ⁶So it was, that while they were there, the days were completed for her to be delivered. ⁷And she brought forth her firstborn Son, and wrapped Him in swaddling cloths, and laid Him in a manger, because there was no room for them in the inn.

Luke 2:1-7

Mary had to trust God at His word when the King sought to kill her son and they had to escape to Egypt to hide for the next 2-3 years.

Now when they had departed, behold, an angel of the Lord appeared to Joseph in a dream, saying, "Arise, take the young Child and His mother, flee to Egypt, and stay there until I bring you word; for Herod will seek the young Child to destroy Him." Matthew 2:13

Mary trusted God and never stopped believing His promise through many hard times and failures. She had to remember what God told her at every turn and disappointment. She had to hold on to what God told her years earlier with a fixed faith-a faith that never stopped believing.

How do we remain fixed in our faith to God's promises when we all we have is His last spoken word and promise?

A Fixed Faith Remembers and Returns to God's Word.

Mary had to remember and consider:

that when she was an unwed pregnant mother with scandal attached to her and her son, that she was *highly favored.*

that when her son had no place to lay his head, hopelessly wandering from town to town that God said that *He will be great.*

that when her son had to escape from those who wanted to kill him that God said *He is the Son of the Highest.*

that when she was taunted that her son was a liar and a fraud, that God said that of His Kingdom, *there will be no end.*

that when they plotted to betray her son that God said He would *give Him the Throne.*

that when she witnessed her innocent son die on a cursed cross that God promised that He would *reign on the throne of Jacob forever.*

A Fixed Faith Never Stops Believing

Like Mary, we must never stop believing in an all-powerful God. She never stopped or failed in her faith, and she saw God's promise fulfilled.

She never stopped believing despite the fact that this promised child may have looked like any other average child, possibly less, in appearance.

She never stopped believing when the ups and downs of childhood happened to him as it did any other child.

She never stopped believing when the rumor and the shame of the nature of his birth continued to surround him.

She never stopped believing when she had to sacrifice the expectations of her life and standing in her community.

She never stopped believing despite the contradiction of watching him persecuted, stalked, rallied against, falsely accused, beaten beyond recognition, and murdered without a cause.

Yet because she believed, she saw a completion of what she was promised. She witnessed the resurrection of her son and His ascension back to His throne, knowing that He would return on His gloriously appointed day.

Mary's Poem

Me. He created me

Me. He chose me.

Me. He blessed me.

Me who no one noticed

Me who no one liked

I was made into a miracle

Giving birth to the light

I never stopped believing

For He spoke into My Dreams

He sang sweet songs of life and love

Filling my heart, busting at the seams

For when life turned gray

With winds of hurt and shame

I remembered what He told me

And trusted through the pain

I did not understand it all
I could not see it clear
But when I held my son
I knew that God was near

He was near
When I was ashamed
Of a strange and lonely son

He was near
When my son told me
That he and God were one

He was near
when they took him
to hang upon a tree

He was near
when He died
For all the world to see

With pain so severe

That I could not breathe

I remember the dream

And I still believed

I never stopped believing

When my son was crushed

That He chose me

To birth God with us

Me. He created me

Me. He chose me.

Me. He blessed me.

Me who no one noticed

Me who no one liked

I was made into a miracle

Giving birth to the light

By *E. Greene*

Personal Reflection

Whether you feel that you are average or even below average or whether you feel that your life has been less than ideal, know that you have an identity in God.

Life and its circumstances have often stolen our identity and sense of value. This can make some feel forsaken and alone, like a helpless victim of life. Others may fight back at the seeming unfairness of life, finding their own identities or sense of value, yet not understanding why that void inside of them is never filled.

Like Mary, God wants to affirm who you are to Him. Your identity in Him looks nothing like the person you may see in the mirror. Nor does His story for you match what you have told about yourself.

In order to find our identity and have our lives authored by God, we must not let go of His promise. We must not let go of His truths when everything around us has declared the opposite. In time and in season, God will complete the work of you, the book of you, if you never stop believing in the God of your promise.

If you can hold on to Him, the author and finisher of your faith, He will leave no promise unfinished. He will not leave you undone but will perform all He has ordained for you.

Can you, like Mary, accept and believe that He has esteemed and favored you?

Can you respond to the Lord with a resounding yes to His will in your life and trust that He will keep His promise?

Can you begin to rejoice now for blessings and promises to come, not only for you but for the countless generations that will be blessed by your testimony?

Like Mary, you will be abundantly blessed when you believe and live your life according to that belief in the God of your promise.

And blessed is she that believed for there shall be a performance of those things which were told her from the Lord. Luke 1:45

Prayer

Lord Jesus, I choose to believe. I choose to fix my faith in Your word, Your truth, and Your promises. For I am your beloved daughter, highly favored, and blessed. Whatever you have for me, I accept. Whatever you desire from me, I give. However, you use me, I submit. For You are God and Your promises are always yes and always amen.

I rebuke the devourer of my hope and faith. When I am tempted to find my answers elsewhere, Lord, raise your word as a standard before me. Shine the light of Your truth on my situation and circumstance and lead me step by step in Your way.

Lord Jesus, I need Your affirmation. Show me my identity.

Lord, I need your protection. Let me feel your presence all around me and strengthen me with your right hand.

Lord Jesus, I need your love. Give me a deeper revelation of your love for me and cast fear far from me.

Give me a faith for the things I cannot see so that I may one day open my eyes to see every one of Your promises fulfilled.

In Jesus Name. Amen.

A letter from the Author and Finisher of your faith.

Your story is my story.

Before you were conceived, I carried your story in my heart. I witnessed all that was good and all that was bad before you took your first breath. I declared your name and identity and placed a record of it on the walls of my heart. I fashioned you uniquely, pondering the balance of you, the extreme of you and delicately placed your pieces together in my hands. I kissed you and gave you breath, placing you in a chosen womb.

As I watched you grow and develop, I delighted in how your pieces turned in to a masterpiece. I beamed with pride when your essence showed through in your thoughts, expressions, and opinions. I danced and sang over you when I witnessed your gifts and talents glimmer and shine through.

Yes, your life is a story that I am writing. Every chapter is linked to the next chapter. Regardless of the twists and turns in the plot of your life, I am faithful to your story and the completion of my work.

Yet, your role is not passive. You have a part to play and a place to write in your story. For I can take it all and weave a tapestry that tells a beautiful tale of My love and faithfulness to you.

With every plot, there is an antagonist. An enemy to thwart the plans and destiny of your story. With ink of doubt and shame, his plan is to turn you into a fallen hero, a tainted princess, an impotent warrior, and a barren and bitter vessel. The earlier he inserts his plot the more tangled your story becomes, like a maze of endless dead ends.

However, as your Creator and God, I know how he tangled your destiny and twisted your plot. So, I have come to show you the way, to show you the open and straight path to your destiny, and to help you finish your race.

For, I know where the dead ends are located. I have experienced the detours and stalls. I have felt the frustration of tight spaces. For, I have already gone before you and lived your story. I found the crossroad and opened the path to freedom, marking it with my body and My blood. For I am the Author of your life and I will complete the work that I started long ago.

If you want to know who you are and why you are here, can you trust Me with the plot of your life? Can you give Me the broken story and twisted plots that have distorted your identity and perverted your destiny?

Allow Me to blot out the sin and the shame with My blood that I shed for you.

Know that I love you. Know that I have gone through all that you have experienced, in order to make a way for you to come out victorious. Know that all stories will glorify Me and display My will and sovereignty in creation, whether one submits their pen and paper to it or not.

Will you let me engrave your true story in My book? Will you place your pen in My hands to write your true story?

I will make your story good. I will make your story holy. I will fill your story with My love and bind it with My sacrifice.

So, today reject the false story. Like Tamar, accept that I have given you a name and a purpose and a holy story to walk in.

Today, give Me your strengths and weakness. Like Rahab, trust Me with all of your effort, resources, and talents even in the face of fear, doubt, and confusion.

Today, seek to know My heart and learn My love. Like Ruth, give what you do not have. Pour out that which you thirst. Nourish others in your weakness and let Me pour my love back into you; a love that never runs dry, a love that brings life in the overflow.

Today, reach for Me in your prison. Call upon Me in the pit of your despair. Hold on to My promise while standing on the ledge of desperation. Like Bathsheba, let Me show you the purpose for the pain and the promise in the prison.

Today, believe Me. Believe that I am who I say that I am, and I will do what I say I will do. Believe that I am true. Believe that I am faithful. Believe that I have all power. Believe that I am never late. Like Mary, believe that you are favored and blessed. Never let go of your faith even in the face of contradiction, delay, death, or destruction.

It is My desire to stand with you at the last chapter of your life to show you My love and faithfulness at every season and how I took it all and made it good.

For in My story dwells your story and with the ink of My blood and Spirit, I am writing the Book of You.

Song "The Book of You"

lyrics by Ericka Greene & music by Javion Duncan

https://soundcloud.com/user-787115465/book-of-you-fmt

Designed in my mind

Fashioned in my heart

You are a masterpiece

A completed work from the start

Created for divine purpose

Each part perfectly placed

A reflection of my glory

In me, there are no mistakes

I'm rewriting the chapters that did not flow

I'm preserving the plot ordained long ago

I'm taking the twists and turns

And making them good

I've bound the pages forever with nail and wood

The pages of your life may be tattered

The chapters, stained through and through

In my hands your story is Holy

With ink of blood and spirit, I'm writing the Book of You

CPSIA information can be obtained
at www.ICGtesting.com
Printed in the USA
LVHW072150050721
691876LV00027B/4347